Love, Mom + Dad
2021

CONGRATULATIONS, GRADUATE!

You proved you're smart.
Now go change the world!

Published by Sellers Publishing, Inc.
161 John Roberts Road, South Portland, Maine 04106
www.sellerspublishing.com • E-mail: rsp@rsvp.com

Cover design by Patti Urban
Interior design by Faceout Studio

ISBN 13: 978-1-4162-4573-5
Library of Congress Control Number: 2015947979

10 9 8 7 6 5 4 3 2

Printed in the United States of America.

Note: *Congratulations, Graduate!* is an expanded and updated edition of the previously published *Creating a Life You'll Love* (2009, Sellers Publishing, Inc.).

Credits: Page 304

Words of Wisdom from Notable Achievers

CONGRATULATIONS, GRADUATE!

You proved you're smart.
Now go change the world!

Edited by Mark Evan Chimsky

SELLERS
PUBLISHING

Contents

Molly Ivins's popular nationally syndicated column appeared in more than 400 newspapers and she was the author of the best seller *Who Let the Dogs In?* In her 2003 commencement address at Scripps College, she encourages everyone "to get out there and raise hell about damned near everything."

Three-time Pulitzer Prize–winner Thomas L. Friedman is the author of such celebrated best sellers as *Hot, Flat and Crowded* and *The World Is Flat*. In his 2005 commencement address at Williams College, he emphasizes the importance of "doing what you really love to do" and cultivating the "ability to learn how to learn."

With sardonic wit and incisive social critiques, David Sedaris has become one of America's preemient humor writers. In his 2006 commencement address at Princeton University, he ponders what happens when you don't pursue the "double major" your parents had been counting on you to complete.

Anna Deavere Smith has created searing portraits of a multitude of characters in her one-woman plays that reflect the pulse of our times. In her 2007 commencement address at Bates College, she urges us to step out of the comfort zone of "safe," accepted identity to discover "the crossroads of ambiguity."

Karen Tse

You Are Not Alone

Honored for her work worldwide as a human rights advocate, Karen Tse is the founder and CEO of International Bridges to Justice, which promotes systemic global change in the administration of criminal justice. In her 2007 commencement address at Scripps College, she describes how life has taught her a powerful truth: that as we begin to change the world, we, ourselves, "are transformed as well."

Ian McEwan

Speaking Freely

Widely recognized as one of the masters of contemporary literature, Ian McEwan is the author of fourteen novels, including *Amsterdam* and *Atonement*, and two collections of stories. In his 2015 commencement address at Dickinson College, he takes a thought-provoking look at how "freedom of expression sustains all the other freedoms we enjoy" and that "without free speech, democracy is a sham."

Genevieve Bell

"Be Naked as Often as Possible": Anthropological Advice

Genevieve Bell is a Vice President and Intel Fellow in the Corporate Strategy Office at Intel. In her 2008 commencement address at UC Berkeley School of Information, Dr. Bell illuminates the "four ways of being" that will be invaluable for experiencing the world.

Ray Kurzweil

What the Future Will Bring

Ray Kurzweil is one of the leading pioneers in the field of artificial intelligence. In his 2005 commencement address at Worcester Polytechnic Institute, he offers a look at the "three great revolutions" that will have a major impact on our lives.

Introduction

"Stuff comes up. Weird doors open. People fall into things," says humor writer David Sedaris in his hilarious commencement address. Dr. Kathryn D. Sullivan, the first American woman to walk in space, puts it this way in her speech, "Do not be afraid of change. Like gravity, it's kind of everywhere; resistance is futile." In this book of 21 of the best and most inspiring commencement addresses, one of the themes is: *expect the unexpected.* Take a turn even if you don't quite know where it leads. It might get you where you didn't even know you wanted to go.

Congratulations, Graduate! is a book that will be fun and illuminating for all new graduates who are about to set off on their own for the first time. As I put this collection together, I culled through a wide array of speeches in search of the ones that said something unique or provocative. I felt like one of those prospectors in the Old West who sift patiently and are ultimately rewarded with nuggets that gleam gold.

The 21 commencement addresses in this book cover a wide spectrum of fascinating themes and ideas by a diverse group of luminaries. All of them share insights about finding one's own path in life and the importance of caring about others and the planet. They call for you to take a stand and advise you not to take yourself too seriously. They discuss the value of community and warn of the dangers of conformity. They exhort you to change the world and to remember to thank the folks who made it possible for you to do it.

Within these pages you will find a treasure trove of life lessons that will entertain and enlighten you. The notable achievers in this book share their hard-earned wisdom about how to live a life that is purposeful and meaningful.

- Read Arianna Huffington on making time to disconnect from technology and "reconnect with yourself."

- Spend time with Ian McEwan's speech on the value of preserving the "sometimes inconvenient and even offensive culture of freedom of expression we have."

- Take an extra moment to meditate on Wendell Berry's words as he urges us toward "responsible citizenship" and says we "must refuse to accept the common delusion that a career is an adequate context for a life."

- Think about ways to follow Anna Deavere Smith's advice to "come out of your safe houses of identity . . . where there is no house, where it is not safe."

- Take heed when Anne Lamott counsels, "You are not your bank account or your ambitiousness" and that we all need to learn "how to feed and nourish our spirit, and the spirit of others."

- Delight in Tess Gerritsen's five "creepy facts" that provide universal truths to live by.

- Take heart in Barbara Kingsolver's celebration of hope and the need to reach out to others: "You are beautiful. You can be as earnest and ridiculous as you need to be, if you don't attempt it in isolation. The magic is community."

From Tom Hanks on the importance of choosing to provide help "on any given day, in any given cause," to Karen Tse on being part of the "human rights revolution," to David McCullough on the need to "make the love of learning central to your life," the 21 contributors to *Congratulations, Graduate!* reveal the ways to connect with your own humanity as you find your unique place in the world. More wonderful discoveries await you in every one of the commencement addresses in this book. I like to think that each of you will find particular pieces that speak directly to you and resonate with your own circumstances and experiences. Delve into these commencement addresses and you'll find lessons that will surprise you, uplift you, and yes, even make you laugh — sometimes all in the same speech!

Like beacon stars that help travelers navigate through the darkness, these commencement addresses will hopefully give you valuable waypoints for the road ahead. Think of this book as a GPS for life after college — not just to help you figure out where you want to go, but also to help you be who you want to be along the way.

So, congratulations, graduate! May this book be a helpful guide as you begin the next step of your exciting journey.

Happy reading!

Mark Evan Chimsky
October 2015

How to be Hopeful

Barbara Kingsolver

BARBARA KINGSOLVER is the acclaimed author of novels, short fiction, nonfiction, and poetry. Her work includes the best-selling *Flight Behavior*; *Animal, Vegetable, Miracle*; *Prodigal Summer*; *The Poisonwood Bible*; *Pigs in Heaven*; *Animal Dreams*; and *The Bean Trees*. Her books have earned major literary awards at home and abroad, and in 2000 she received the National Humanities Medal, our nation's highest honor for service through the arts. In 1997 Ms. Kingsolver established the PEN/Bellwether Prize, awarded in even-numbered years to a first novel that exemplifies outstanding literary quality and a commitment to literature as a tool for social change.

How to be Hopeful

BARBARA KINGSOLVER

In her 2008 commencement address at Duke University, Barbara Kingsolver reflects on our changing world and why "the happiest people are the ones with the most community."

The very least you can do in your life is to figure out what you hope for. The most you can do is live inside that hope, running down its hallways, touching the walls on both sides.

Let me begin that way: with an invocation of your own best hopes.

What can I say to people who know almost everything? There was a time when I surely knew, because I'd just graduated from college myself, after writing down the sum of all human knowledge on exams and research papers. But that great pedagogical swilling-out must have depleted my reserves, because decades have passed and now I can't believe how much I don't know. Looking back, I can discern a kind of gaseous exchange in which I exuded cleverness and gradually absorbed better judgment. Wisdom is like frequent-flyer miles and scar tissue; if it does accumulate, that happens by accident while you're trying to do something else. And wisdom is what people will start wanting from you, after your last exam. I know it's true for writers — when people love a book, whatever they say about it, what they really mean is: it was *wise*. It helped explain their pickle. My favorites are the canny old codgers: Neruda, García Márquez, Doris Lessing. Honestly, it is harrowing for me to try to teach twenty-year-old students, who earnestly want to improve their writing. The best I can think to tell them is: Quit smoking, and observe posted speed limits. This will improve your odds of getting old enough to be wise.

So I'll proceed, with a caveat. The wisdom of each generation is necessarily new. This tends to dawn on us in revelatory moments, brought to us by our children. For example: My younger daughter is eleven. Every morning, she and I walk down the lane from our farm to the place where she meets the school bus. It's the best part of my day. We have great conversations. But a few weeks ago as we stood waiting in the dawn's early light, Lily was quietly looking me over, and finally said: "Mom, just so you know, the only reason I'm letting you wear that outfit is because of your age." The *alleged outfit* will not be described here; whatever you're imagining will perfectly suffice. (Especially if you're picturing *Project Runway* meets *Working with Livestock*.) Now, I believe parents should uphold respect for adult authority, so I did what I had to do. I hid behind the barn when the bus came.

And then I walked back up the lane in my fly regalia, contemplating this new equation: "Because of your age." It's okay now to deck out and turn up as the village idiot. Hooray! I am old enough. How does this happen? Over a certain age, do you become invisible? There is considerable evidence for this in movies and television. But mainly, I think, you're not expected to know the rules. Everyone knows you're operating on software that hasn't been updated for a good while.

The world shifts under our feet. The rules change. Not the Bill of Rights, or the rules of tenting, but the big unspoken truths of a generation. Exhaled by culture, taken in like oxygen, we hold these truths to be self-evident: You get what you pay for. Success is everything. Work is what you do for money, and that's what counts. How could it be otherwise? And the converse of that last rule, of course, is that if you're not paid to do a thing, it can't be important. If a child writes a poem and proudly reads it, adults may wink and ask, "Think there's a lot of money in that?" You may also hear this when you declare a major in English. Being a good neighbor, raising children: the road to success is not paved with the likes of these. Some workplaces actually quantify your likelihood of being distracted by family or volunteerism. It's called your coefficient of drag. The ideal number is zero. This is the Rule of Perfect Efficiency.

Now, the rule of "Success" has traditionally meant having boatloads of money. But we are not really supposed to put it in a boat. A house would be the customary thing. Ideally it should be large, with a lot of bathrooms and so forth, but no more than four people. If two friends come over during approved visiting hours, the two children have to leave. The bathroom-to-resident ratio should at all times remain greater than one. I'm not making this up, I'm just observing, it's more or less my profession. As Yogi Berra told us, you can observe a lot just by watching. I see our dream-houses standing alone, the idealized life taking place in a kind of bubble. So you need another bubble, with rubber tires, to convey yourself to places you must visit, such as an office. If you're successful, it will be a large, empty-ish office you don't have to share. If you need anything, you can get it delivered. Play your cards right and you may never have to come face to face with another person. This is the Rule of Escalating Isolation.

And so we find ourselves in the chapter of history I would

entitle: Isolation and Efficiency, and How They Came Around to Bite Us in the Backside. Because it's looking that way. We're a world at war, ravaged by disagreements, a bizarrely globalized people in which the extravagant excesses of one culture wash up as famine or flood on the shores of another. Even the architecture of our planet is collapsing under the weight of our efficient productivity. Our climate, our oceans, migratory paths, things we believed were independent of human affairs. Twenty years ago, climate scientists first told Congress that unlimited carbon emissions were building toward a disastrous instability. Congress said, we need to think about that. About ten years later, nations of the world wrote the Kyoto Protocol, a set of legally binding controls on our carbon emissions. The U.S. said, we still need to think about it. Now we can watch as glaciers disappear, the lights of biodiversity go out, the oceans reverse their ancient orders. A few degrees looked so small on the thermometer. We are so good at measuring things and declaring them under control. How could our weather turn murderous, pummel our coasts and push new diseases like dengue fever onto our doorsteps? It's an emergency on a scale we've never known. We've responded by following the rules we know: Efficiency, Isolation. We can't slow down our productivity and consumption, that's unthinkable. Can't we just go home and put a really big lock on the door?

Not this time. Our paradigm has met its match. The world will save itself, don't get me wrong. The term "fossil fuels" is not a metaphor or a simile. In the geological sense, it's over. The internal combustion engine is so twentieth-century. Now we can either shift away from a carbon-based economy, or find another place to live. Imagine it: we raised you on a lie. Everything you plug in, turn on or drive, the out-of-season foods you eat, the music in your ears. We gave you this world and promised you could keep it running on: *a fossil substance.* Dinosaur slime, and it's running out. The geologists only disagree on how much is left, and the climate scientists are now saying they're sorry but that's not even the point. We won't get time to use it all. To stabilize the floods and firestorms, we'll have to reduce our carbon emissions by 80 percent, within a decade.

Heaven help us get our minds around that. We're still stuck on a strategy of bait-and-switch: Okay, we'll keep the cars but run them on ethanol made from corn! But . . . we use petroleum to grow the corn. Even if you like the idea of robbing the food bank to fill up the tank, there is a math problem: it takes nearly a gallon of fossil fuel to render an equivalent gallon of corn gas. By some accounts, it takes more. Think of the Jules Verne novel in which the hero is racing Around the World in 80 Days, and finds himself stranded in the mid-Atlantic on a steamship that's run out of coal. It's day 79. So Phileas Fogg convinces the Captain to pull up the decks and throw them into the boiler. "On the next day the masts, rafts and spars were burned. The crew worked lustily, keeping up the fires. There was a perfect rage for demolition." The Captain remarked, "Fogg, you've got something of the Yankee about you." Oh, novelists. They always manage to have the last word, even when they are dead.

How can we get from here to there, without burning up our ship? That will be the central question of your adult life: to escape the wild rumpus of carbon-fuel dependency, in the nick of time. You'll make rules that were previously unthinkable, imposing limits on what we can use and possess. You will radically reconsider the power relationship between humans and our habitat. In the words of my esteemed colleague and friend, Wendell Berry, the new Emancipation Proclamation will not be for a specific race or species, but for life itself. Imagine it. Nations have already joined together to rein in global consumption. Faith communities have found a new point of agreement with student activists, organizing around the conviction that caring for our planet is a moral obligation. Before the last UN Climate Conference in Bali, thousands of U.S. citizens contacted the State Department to press for binding limits on carbon emissions. We're the 5 percent of humans who have made 50 percent of all the greenhouse gases up there. But our government is reluctant to address it, for one reason: it might hurt our economy.

For a lot of history, many nations said exactly the same thing about abolishing slavery. We can't grant humanity to all people, it would hurt our cotton plantations, our sugar crop, our balance of trade. Until the daughters and sons of a new wisdom declared: We don't care. You have to find another way. Enough of this shame.

Have we lost that kind of courage? Have we let economic growth become our undisputed master again? As we track the unfolding disruption of natural and global stabilities, you will be told to buy into business as usual: You need a job. Trade your future for an entry-level position. Do what we did, preserve a profitable climate for manufacture and consumption, at any cost. Even at the cost of the other climate — the one that was hospitable to life as we knew it. Is anyone thinking this through? In the awful moment when someone demands at gunpoint, "Your money or your life," that's not supposed to be a hard question.

A lot of people, in fact, are rethinking the money answer. Looking behind the cash-price of everything, to see what it cost us elsewhere: to mine and manufacture, to transport, to burn, to bury. What did it harm on its way here? Could I get it closer to home? Previous generations rarely asked about the hidden costs. We put them on layaway. You don't get to do that. The bill has come due. Some European countries already are calculating the "climate cost" on consumer goods and adding it to the price. The future is here. We're examining the moralities of possession, inventing renewable technologies, recovering sustainable food systems. We're even warming up to the idea that the wealthy nations will have to help the poorer ones, for the sake of a reconstructed world. We've done it before. That was the Marshall Plan. Generosity is not out of the question. It will grind some gears in the machine of Efficiency. But we can retool.

We can also rethink the big, lonely house as a metaphor for success. You are in a perfect position to do that. For those of you who may have just graduated from college, you've probably spent very little of your recent life in a freestanding unit with a bathroom-to-resident ratio of greater than one. (Maybe more like 1:200.) You've been living so close to your friends, you didn't have to ask about their problems, you had to step over them to get into the room. As you moved from dormitory to apartment to whatever, you've had such a full life, surrounded by people, in all kinds of social and physical structures, none of which belonged entirely to you.

You're told that's all about to change. That growing up means leaving the herd, starting up the long escalator to isolation.

Not necessarily. As you venture out into the world, remember what you loved about the way you lived, in close and continuous contact. This is an ancient human social construct that once was common in this land. We called it a community. We lived among our villagers, depending on them for what we needed. If we had a problem, we did not discuss it over the phone with someone in Bhubaneswar. We went to a neighbor. We acquired food from farmers. We listened to music in groups, in churches, or on front porches. We danced. We participated. Even when there was no money in it. Community is our native state. You play hardest for a hometown crowd. You become your best self. You know joy. This is not a guess, there is evidence. The scholars who study social well-being can put it on charts and graphs. In the last thirty years our material wealth has increased in this country, but our self-described happiness has steadily declined. Elsewhere, the people who consider themselves very happy are not in the very poorest nations, as you might guess, nor in the very richest. The winners are Mexico, Ireland, Puerto Rico, the kinds of places we identify with extended family, noisy villages, a lot of dancing. The happiest people are the ones with the most community.

You can take that to the bank. I'm not sure what they'll do

with it down there, but you could try. You could create an unconventionally communal sense of how your life may be. This could be your key to a new order: you don't need so much stuff to fill your life, when you have people in it. You don't need jet fuel to get food from a farmer's market. You could invent a new kind of Success that includes children's poetry, butterfly migrations, butterfly kisses, the Grand Canyon, eternity. If somebody says, "Your money or your life," you could say: Life. And mean it. You'll see things collapse in your time, the big houses, the empires of glass. The new green things that sprout up through the wreck — those will be yours.

The arc of history is longer than human vision. It bends. We abolished slavery, we granted universal suffrage. We have done hard things before. And every time it took a terrible fight between people who could not imagine changing the rules, and those who said, "We already did. We have made the world new." The hardest part will be to convince yourself of the possibilities, and hang on. If you run out of hope at the end of the day, to rise in the morning and put it on again with your shoes. Hope is the only reason you won't give in, burn what's left of the ship and go down with it. The ship of your natural life and your children's only shot. You have to love that so earnestly — you, who were born into the Age of Irony.

Imagine getting caught with your Optimism hanging out. It feels so risky. Like showing up at the bus stop as the village idiot. You may be asked to stand behind the barn. You may feel you're not up to the task.

But think of this: You are beautiful. You can be as earnest and ridiculous as you need to be, if you don't attempt it in isolation. The magic is community. The ridiculously earnest are known to travel in groups. And they are known to change the world. Look at you. That could be you.

I'll close with a poem:

HOPE: AN OWNER'S MANUAL

Look, you might as well know, this thing
is going to take endless repair: rubber bands,
crazy glue, tapioca, the square of the hypotenuse.
Nineteenth-century novels. Heartstrings, sunrise:
all of these are useful. Also, feathers.

To keep it humming, sometimes you have to stand
on an incline, where everything looks possible;
on the line you drew yourself. Or in
the grocery line, making faces at a toddler
secretly, over his mother's shoulder.

You might have to pop the clutch and run
past all the evidence. Past everyone who is
laughing or praying for you. Definitely you don't
want to go directly to jail, but still, here you go,
passing time, passing strange. Don't pass this up.

In the worst of times, you will have to pass it off.
Park it and fly by the seat of your pants. With nothing
in the bank, you'll still want to take the express.
Tiptoe past the dogs of the apocalypse that are sleeping
in the shade of your future. Pay at the window.
Pass your hope like a bad check.
You might still have just enough time. To make a deposit.

The Love of Learning

David McCullough

DAVID McCULLOUGH has twice received the Pulitzer Prize, for *Truman* and *John Adams*, and twice received the National Book Award, for *The Path Between the Seas* and *Mornings on Horseback*. His other widely praised books are *The Wright Brothers*, *1776*, *Brave Companions*, *The Great Bridge*, and *The Johnstown Flood*. He has been honored with the National Book Foundation Distinguished Contribution to American Letters Award, the National Humanities Medal, and the Presidential Medal of Freedom.

The Love of Learning

David McCullough

In his 2008 commencement address at Boston College, David McCullough challenges us to honor "the transforming miracle of education."

The importance of education has been a prevailing theme in American life from the beginning and may it ever be so.

Information. Information at our fingertips. Information without end . . .

The Library of Congress has 650 miles of shelves and books in 470 languages . . . Napoleon was afraid of cats . . . A porcupine is born with 30,000 quills . . . A mosquito beats its wings 600 times per second . . . Coal production in the United States is second only to that of China.

It's said ad infinitum: ours is the Information Age. There's never been anything like it since the dawn of creation. We glory in the Information Highway as other eras gloried in railroads. Information for all! Information night and day!

. . . A column of air a mile square, starting 50 feet from the ground and extending to 14,000 feet contains an average of 25,000,000 insects . . . James Madison weighed less than a hundred pounds, William Howard Taft, 332 pounds, a presidential record . . . According to *The World Almanac*, the length of the index finger on the Statue of Liberty is 8 feet . . . The elevation of the highest mountain in Massachusetts, Mount Greylock, is 3,487 feet . . . The most ancient living tree in America, a bristlecone pine in California, is 4,700 years old . . .

Information is useful. Information is often highly interesting. Information has value, sometimes great value. The right bit of information at the opportune moment can be worth a fortune. Information can save time and effort. Information can save your life. The value of information, facts, figures, and the like, depends on what we make of it — on judgment.

But information, let us be clear, isn't learning. Information isn't poetry. Or art. Or Gershwin or the Shaw Memorial. Or faith. It isn't wisdom. Facts alone are never enough. Facts rarely if ever have any soul. In writing or trying to understand history one may have all manner of "data," and miss the point. One can have all the facts and miss the truth. It can be like the old piano teacher's lament to her student, "I hear all the notes, but I hear no music."

If information were learning, you could memorize *The World Almanac* and call yourself educated. If you memorized *The World Almanac*, you wouldn't be educated. You'd be weird!

Learning is not to be found on a printout. It's not on call at the touch of the finger. Learning is acquired mainly from books, and most readily from great books. And from teachers, and the more learned and empathetic the better. And from work, concentrated work.

Abigail Adams put it perfectly more than two hundred years ago: "Learning is not attained by chance. It must be sought with ardor and attended with diligence." Ardor, to my mind, is the key word.

For many of you, the love of learning may have already taken hold. For others it often happens later and often by surprise, as history has shown time and again. That's part of the magic.

Consider the example of Charles Sumner, the great Senator Charles Sumner of Massachusetts, whose statue stands in the Boston Public Garden facing Boylston Street.

As a boy in school Charles Sumner had shown no particular promise. Nor did he distinguish himself as an undergraduate at Harvard. He did love reading, however, and by the time he finished law school, something overcame him. Passionate to know more, learn more, he put aside the beginnings of a law practice and sailed for France on his own and on borrowed money, in order to attend lectures at the Sorbonne. It was a noble adventure in independent scholarship, if ever there was. Everything was of interest to him. He attended lectures on natural history, geology, Egyptology, criminal law, the history of philosophy, and pursued a schedule of classical studies that would have gladdened the heart of the legendary Father Thayer of Boston College. He attended lectures at the Paris medical schools. He went to the opera, the theater, the Louvre, all the while pouring out his excitement in the pages of his journal and in long letters home. Trying to express what he felt on seeing the works of Raphael and Leonardo da Vinci at the Louvre, he wrote, "They touched my mind, untutored as it is, like a rich strain of music."

But there was more. Something else touched him deeply. At lectures at the Sorbonne he had observed how black students were perfectly at ease with and well received by the other students. The color of one's skin seemed to make no difference. Sumner was pleased to see this, though at first it struck him as strange. But then he thought, as he wrote, that maybe the "distance" between blacks and whites at home was something white Americans had been taught and that "does not exist in the nature of things."

And therein was the seed from which would later arise, in the 1850s, before the Civil War, Charles Sumner's strident stand on the floor of the United States Senate against the spread of slavery. From his quest for learning he brought home a personal revelation he had not anticipated and it changed history.

But perhaps, overall, John Adams is as shining an example of the transforming miracle of education as we have. John Adams came from the humblest of beginnings. His father was a plain Braintree farmer and shoemaker. His mother was almost certainly illiterate. Because a scholarship made possible a college education, the boy discovered books. "I discovered books and read forever," he later wrote and it was hardly an exaggeration. At age eighty, we know, he was happily embarking on a sixteen-volume history of France.

When I set out to write the life of John Adams, I wanted not only to read what he and Abigail wrote, but to read as much as possible of what they read. We're all what we read to a very considerable degree.

So there I was past age sixty taking up once again, for the first time since high school and college English classes, the essays of Samuel Johnson and works of Pope, Swift, and Laurence Sterne. I read Samuel Richardson's *Clarissa*, which was Abigail's favorite novel; and Cervantes — *Don Quixote* — for the first time in my life. What a joy!

Cervantes is part of us, whether we know it or not. Declare you're in a pickle; talk of birds of a feather flocking together; vow to turn over a new leaf; give the devil his due, or insist that mum's the word, and you're quoting Cervantes every time.

"I cannot live without books," Thomas Jefferson wrote to Adams late in life, knowing Adams would understand perfectly. Adams read everything — Shakespeare and the Bible over and over, and the Psalms especially. He read poetry, fiction, history. Always carry a book with you on your travels he advised his son, John Quincy. "You will never be alone with a poet in your pocket."

In a single year, according to the U.S. Department of Education, among all Americans with a college education, fully a third read not one novel or short story or poem. Don't be one of those.

Make the love of learning central to your life. What a difference it can mean. If your experience is anything like mine, the books that will mean the most to you, books that will change your life, are still to come. And remember, as someone said, even the oldest book is brand new for the reader who opens it for the first time.

Read. Read, read! Read the classics of American literature that you've never opened. Read your country's history. How can we profess to love our country and take no interest in its history? Read into the history of Greece and Rome. Read about the great turning points in the history of science and medicine and ideas.

Read for pleasure, to be sure. I adore a good thriller or a first-rate murder mystery. But take seriously — read closely — books that have stood the test of time. Study a masterpiece, take it apart, study its architecture, its vocabulary, its intent. Underline, make notes in the margins, and after a few years, go back and read it again.

Make use of the public libraries. Start your own personal library and see it grow. Talk about the books you're reading. Ask others what they're reading. You'll learn a lot.

And please, please, do what you can to cure the verbal virus that seems increasingly rampant among your generation. I'm talking about the relentless, wearisome use of the words, "like," and "you know," and "awesome," and "actually." Listen to yourselves as you speak.

Just imagine if in his inaugural address John F. Kennedy had said, "Ask not what your country can, you know, do for you, but what you can, like, do for your country actually."

The energetic part so many of you are playing in this year's presidential race is marvelous. Keep at it, down to the wire. Keep that idealism alive. Make a difference. Set an example for all of us.

Go out and get the best jobs you can and go to work with spirit. Don't get discouraged. And don't work just for money. Choose work you believe in, work you enjoy. Money enough will follow. Believe me, there's nothing like turning to every day to do work you love.

Walk with your heads up. And remember, honesty is the best policy; and yes that, too, is from Cervantes.

Travel as much as you can, and wherever you go, before checking out of a hotel or motel, always remember to tip the maid.

In the words of the immortal Jonathan Swift, "May you live all the days of your life."

On we go.

On Our Relationship with Technology, with the World, and with Ourselves

Arianna Huffington

ARIANNA HUFFINGTON is the Co-Founder, President, and Editor-in-Chief of The Huffington Post and author of fourteen books. In May 2005, she launched The Huffington Post, a news and blog site that quickly became one of the most widely read, linked to, and frequently cited media brands on the Internet. In 2012, the site won a Pulitzer Prize for national reporting. She has been named to *Time Magazine's* list of the world's one hundred most influential people and the *Forbes* Most Powerful Women list. Originally from Greece, she moved to England when she was sixteen and graduated from Cambridge University with an M.A. in economics. At twenty-one, she became president of the famed debating society, the Cambridge Union. Her fourteenth book, *Thrive: The Third Metric to Redefining Success and Creating a Life of Well-Being, Wisdom, and Wonder* debuted at #1 on the *New York Times* Best Seller list and was released in paperback in March 2015.

On Our Relationship with Technology, with the World, and with Ourselves

ARIANNA HUFFINGTON

In her 2015 commencement address at Vassar College, Arianna Huffington proposes "digital detoxes" as a way to "disconnect from the jumble and the cacophony and make time to reconnect with yourself."

Commencement is one of my favorite rituals — coming together for one last time, dressed alike before you head off into your singular and unique lives. When I was deciding what to wear under my gown, I asked Siri what the weather was in Poughkeepsie. And Siri responded with a list of mixed drinks with whiskey. I think I'm going to wait until Siri comes up with an update for Greek accents.

Today is the culmination of your time at Vassar. And it's also a mini-culmination for me. Because I've spent a lot of time in recent weeks getting to know you — following you and your activities on social media, on Vassar's Web site, in *The Miscellany News*, and in other ways I'm not prepared to disclose that will remain between me and the folks at the NSA. It feels a little like I've been checking out your online dating profile, and now we're finally meeting. And when I saw you walk in, all 611 of you, I breathed a huge sigh of relief. Because let's face it, you look fantastic. If we were on Tinder, I would definitely be ready to swipe right. Or is it left? Actually, at my age, it doesn't matter, as long as you're swiping.

One of the things I learned from my cyber-stalking is that the Vassar College seal shows the goddess Athena in front of the Parthenon, which I love. Though it occurs to me that I'm probably here because Athena couldn't be booked, so you settled for another Greek lady from Athens. And to really sell it, I'll be delivering my speech in a thick, sometimes-hard-to-understand Greek accent, instead of the crystal clear, accentless voice I use at all other times. In my private detective work, I also learned that your former motto "purity and wisdom" was abandoned in 1930, which was probably a good idea given that when *The Miscellany News* — or the *Misc* as I understand you call it — sent out an email to seniors asking what was on their bucket list, most of the answers had to do with sex. One replied, "Have sex under the sex tree!" Another said, "Have sex in the circle couches near the Art Library." A third wrote back, "Sex in the meditation room or the roof of the library." Aren't you glad I'm not disclosing your names in front of your parents? You owe me!

What was clear from all my private detective work is that you belong to a community. And for the rest of your lives, you'll essentially have a language you speak that no one else understands . . . sort of a more fun version of how I've been feeling my whole life. Chili Wednesdays at The Retreat. The Bell Ringing. Founder's Day. Mug Nights. A Quidditch team, The Butterbeer Brooers. The Deece. Running naked through the library the night before final exams. The Vassar Devil, which I understand to be some sort of ice cream sensation I'm definitely planning to sample before I leave. The a cappella groups — all 3,475 of them.

And what a treasure trove of stories you're leaving Vassar with. Not just from your years here but from Vassar's incredibly colorful past: Way back in the 1880s, you invented fudge — maybe. Some of you actually believe that the squirrels around campus are the slightly deranged reincarnations of English majors who couldn't get jobs after graduation. But, hey, at least the squirrels aren't living at home, right mom and dad? And here is my favorite: before your time, Vassar students were given the emblem of an acorn to display on their doors when they did not wish to be disturbed. The custom was apparently discontinued, but I want to urge you to revive it as something to use physically and spiritually for the rest of your lives. It's actually central to the three relationships I want to talk to you about today. And those are: your relationship with technology, your relationship with yourself, and your relationship with the world.

Let's start with your relationship with technology. No generation has been as liberated and as connected by technology as yours. But also, no generation has been as enslaved and as distracted by technology. So bring on that acorn because as the writer Eric Barker said, "Those who can sit in a chair, undistracted for hours, mastering subjects and creating things will rule the world — while the rest of us frantically and futilely try to keep up with texts, tweets and other incessant interruptions." Sadly, we have become not just distracted by our devices, our texts, emails, constant notifications, and social media, but addicted to them. And when it comes to social media, let me break it to you: our addiction is not a bug, but a feature. This isn't some unforeseen side effect, it was always the intention, that social media would consume as much of our time and attention — as much of our lives — as possible.

To your credit, many of you have already recognized this and have taken steps to curb this addiction. As senior Justin Mitchell told the *Misc*, "I was mindlessly going through people's profiles and being an idiot. So I cut it out. There's just not enough time to do that with school." And having graduated just a few years before you, I can tell you there is even less time to do that with life.

But the addiction is so powerful that, according to a recent survey, 20 percent of millennials actually use their smartphones during sex. Maybe I should have read the instructions on my phone more carefully, but I'm not even sure what that means. Indeed, a recent study shows that more than half of women would rather go a month with no sex than a month with no smartphone — although I am sure this survey did not include any women with access to the Vassar Sex Tree.

Contrary to what many of you may think, not only is multitasking not very efficient, it doesn't actually exist. It's actually rapid task switching — instead of doing two things at once, we simply switch between doing two things badly. It's one of the most stressful ways we can use our time, and it robs us of our capacity to notice and appreciate every moment of our lives. I live in New York, and you hardly ever see anybody simply walking down the street who's not also staring at a screen, talking on the phone, or, even worse, texting while walking. It's like being in a really boring zombie movie. I used to be exactly like that myself. I remember one day, I left my apartment with a friend. I looked up and said, "What a gorgeous building! I wonder when that went up?" "1890," my friend said. I'd never noticed it. As Vassar alum Mary Oliver put it, "Instructions for living a life: Pay attention. Be astonished. Tell about it." And by the way, when you do, please tell about it on The Huffington Post. I'm going to make it super easy for you by giving you my email so you can bypass the growing HuffPost blogging bureaucracy: arianna@huffingtonpost.com.

As someone who runs a 24/7 digital media company and who uses every form of social media ever invented, I hope I have some street cred when I urge you to build boundaries, introduce digital detoxes into your life, and learn to regularly disconnect from the jumble and the cacophony and make time to reconnect with yourself. There will be many profound and fulfilling relationships ahead of you, but the relationship with yourself is the most important relationship you'll ever have. And, like any relationship, it can't be taken for granted — without care and attention, it will atrophy and, ultimately, break down.

If there is one thing I wish I knew when I was sitting where you are today — and by the way, there are many — it's that the Delphic admonition "Know Thyself" and Socrates' admonition that "the unexamined life is not worth living" are not ancient philosophical platitudes, but in fact the most relevant and important guiding truths for our lives. In the well-earned rush and excitement of your new life that's about to begin, it's remarkably easy to forget that most important relationship. That's because the ever-increasing creep of technology — into our bedrooms, our brains, and our lives — makes it much harder to connect with ourselves.

Indeed, for so many of us, connecting with ourselves has been so neglected that we will do anything to avoid it. Researchers from Harvard and the University of Virginia did an experiment in which they gave people a choice to be alone in a room, without anything — no devices, no papers, no phones — or get an electric shock. A whopping 67 percent of men chose the electric shock. I'm very happy to say that only 25 percent of women chose the shock. Seriously guys — and a quarter of women — what is wrong with you? It's not like you have to go shopping with your own thoughts or move in with them and pick out drapes, just be alone with them for fifteen minutes. Is it that bad?

In fact most of us actually know more about the state of our smartphones than we do about the state of ourselves. I bet pretty much everyone here knows approximately how much battery remains in your smartphone right now. And when it gets below 20 percent, giving us the dreaded red low power alert, we begin to get anxious and desperately look around for one of the little recharging shrines we meticulously maintain everywhere around us, lest anything should happen to our precious phone. But how much do you know, how aware are you, how mindful are you, of the state of your own being? Of your own energy and alertness and reserves? How quickly do you spring into action when you go into the low power zone?

I was fascinated to read about Vassar's Maria Mitchell, America's first female astronomer, and to see the gorgeous building that used to house her observatory. And while I completely understand the sense of wonder that has led men and women through the ages to explore outer space, I'm personally much more fascinated with exploring inner space. As Thomas Merton put it, "What can we gain by sailing to the moon if we are not able to cross the abyss that separates us from ourselves? This is the most important of all voyages of discovery, and without it all thc rest are not only useless but disastrous." In other words, it's the quality of our inner journeys that allows us to make sense of our outer journeys.

There is now a collective longing to stop living in the shallows and recognize that life is actually shaped from the inside out — a truth that has been celebrated by spiritual teachers, poets, and philosophers throughout the ages and has now been unambiguously validated by modern science. And you, Vassar graduates, can lead the way, and chart a new path forward. You're the first generation born into the digital world. And you can be the first generation to master it, to make it serve you, instead of the other way around. And when you do, you'll find that you have the wind at your back because that's what the times are calling for.

One of the things that's so special about Vassar is that at the heart of your education is a deep and profound sense of responsibility for the world and those around us. You've been taught to use your considerable talents, and your drive and your dedication to make a difference in the world. I was moved and inspired by all the projects you've started and been involved in: The Vassar Prison Initiative, The Vassar Haiti Project, The College Committee on Sustainability, Operation Donation, etc., etc. You've already made a difference in the world you're about to enter.

And it's no accident that Vassar has recognized the crisis of growing inequality in our country. In fact, congratulations for being the number-one college to enroll high-performing, low-income students and support them through successful graduation. The concern about growing inequality has become almost universal — transcending political parties and ideologies. The statistics are staggering: Student loan debt is at 1.2 trillion dollars, the number of Americans in poverty has grown by 15 million since 2000, the number of high-poverty neighborhoods has tripled since 1970, while America is now home to more prisoners than any other country in the world, with more than 2 million people behind bars.

As we see this happening, I keep being reminded of my visit to Pompeii, whose people were wiped out in the first century by a violent volcanic eruption. There had been many warning signs, including a severe earthquake, tremors, springs and wells that dried up, dogs that ran away, and birds that no longer sang. And then the most obvious warning sign: columns of smoke belching out of Mount Vesuvius before the volcano blew its top, burying the city and its inhabitants under sixty feet of ash and volcanic rock. But the warning signs had been dismissed as "not particularly alarming." The warning signs are all around us today, too, pointing out the gulf between what we know we should be doing and what we're choosing to do instead.

It's not that we don't have enough data — in fact, we're drowning in data. What we're lacking is wisdom. Indeed 90 percent of the data now available to us has been created in the last two years. But how much of our collective wisdom has been made available in that time? That's what's missing from our leaders and from our public discourse. Could our political debate, dominated as it is by meaningless head-to-head polls, manufactured controversies, horse-race sound-bites, and news of Hillary Clinton asking for extra guacamole at Chipotle and Ted Cruz suddenly liking country music after 9/11 — be any more trivialized?

In fact, at The Huffington Post we've started a "Who Cares?" section to cover all these non-issues and hopefully leave more room for the real ones. And for those of you going into journalism, our goal at HuffPost is to reimagine the craft. There's an old saying in the news business, one that's guided editorial thinking for decades: "If it bleeds, it leads." But it turns out this is just lousy journalism. As journalists, our job is to provide an accurate picture — and that means the full picture — of what's going on in the world. Just showing tragedy, violence, and mayhem — just focusing on what's broken and what's not working — misses too much of what is really happening all around us. What about how people are responding to these challenges, how they're coming together, even in the midst of violence, poverty, and loss? And what about all the stories of innovation, creativity, ingenuity, compassion, and grace? By shining a light on these stories, we can scale up these solutions and create a positive contagion that can expand and broaden their reach. Instead of just producing copycat crimes, we can start to produce copycat solutions.

And you can be a part of those solutions. There is an invisible but very real and inescapable connection between our relationship with ourselves and our relationship with the world. As Aleksandr Solzhenitsyn put it, "If you wanted to put the world to rights, who should you begin with: yourself or others?" I know everyone here wants to help put the world to rights. But please remember, it begins with yourself . . . as they say on airplanes, secure your own oxygen mask first.

So regularly hang that virtual acorn on your door because while the world will provide plenty of insistent, pleading, flashing, high-volume signals directing you to distract yourself, to not be in the moment, to burn out in order to climb higher up the ladder of what the world defines as success, there will be almost no worldly signals reminding you to stay connected to the essence of who you are, to pause to wonder, and to connect to that place of wisdom in you — that place from which everything is possible. The world will keep coming at you with its incessant demands, beeps, blinking lights, and alerts. "Every day," Iain Thomas wrote, "the world will drag you by the hand, yelling, 'This is important! And this is important! And this is important! You need to worry about this! And this! And this!' And each day, it's up to you to yank your hand back, put it on your heart and say, 'No. This is what's important.'"

It's from this sacred place that life is transformed from struggle to grace, from information to wisdom. We have, if we're lucky, about 30,000 days to play the game of life. And trust me, that's not morbid. In fact, it's wisdom that will put all the inevitable failures and rejections and disappointments and heartbreaks into perspective. Because as the great Onion headline summed it up, "Death Rate Holding Steady at 100%." So let's stop sweeping it under the rug. That's a modern impulse. Ancient Romans would carve "MM," Memento Mori, Remember Death, on statues and trees — to put every victory and every defeat into its proper perspective. I'm not sure if you want to carve it on the sex tree, though, because things could get weird.

And if you've been to a memorial service recently, you'll have noticed that our eulogies have very little to do with our résumés and our LinkedIn profiles. For instance, here's the sort of thing you don't hear in a eulogy: "George was amazing, he increased market share by one-third." Or, "her PowerPoint slides were always meticulously prepared." Or, "she ate lunch at her desk every single day." Our eulogies are always about the other stuff: what we gave, how we connected, how much we meant to our family and friends, small kindnesses, lifelong passions, and the things that made us laugh. So why do we spend so much of our lives chasing things we don't value and that don't ultimately matter?

As you leave this magical campus, don't let technology wrap you up in a perpetually harried existence. Don't be so connected to everybody that you're not truly connected to anybody. Or to yourself. And don't get so caught up in your busy life that life's mystery passes you by. Bring joy and gratitude into every moment — even the tough ones — and start displaying that acorn on your door. Thank you so much.

Go Forth Unafraid

Molly Ivins

MOLLY IVINS was a columnist and political commentator, who was recognized for her lively style, sharp wit, and insight. She was the co-editor of the *Texas Observer* and a reporter for the *New York Times*, the *Dallas Times Herald*, and the *Fort Worth Star-Telegram*. Her nationally syndicated column appeared in more than four hundred newspapers. Her best-selling books included *Who Let the Dogs In?; Bushwhacked* (with Lou Dubose); *Shrub: The Short but Happy Political Life of George W. Bush* (with Lou Dubose); *You Got to Dance With Them What Brung You: Politics in the Clinton Years*; and *Nothin' but Good Times Ahead.* Ms. Ivins died of breast cancer at sixty-two in 2007.

Go Forth Unafraid

Molly Ivins

In her 2003 commencement address at Scripps College, Molly Ivins encourages everyone "to get out there and raise hell about damned near everything."

Go forth unafraid. Actually, given the state of the world, go forth unafraid but probably a soupçon of caution would not be out of place. The other thing I'm supposed to tell you is that success cannot be measured by money; however, in the real world it often is. Money isn't everything, but it helps. Life in the real world is hard, but it is not as hard as Experimental Psychology 2. Education is never wasted, and I bring that up because of my difficulties with experimental psychology. When I got to Experimental Psych, they gave me a Skinner Box and a rat. My rat was supposed to learn that if he pressed the bar, he would get a food pellet. He was a bright rat — he learned that in no time flat. Then, he had to learn that he had to press the bar twice in order to get a food pellet. But, my rat had committed something called overlearning, which can be plotted on a bell curve. And what happened was, he would press once and not get his food pellet, and instead of trying again, my rat developed something called neurotic ritual. It would turn around three times to the left, tossing its little ratty head, and then kind of fall over backwards in frustration. I ruined a perfectly good rat, and felt guilty about it for years and never saw any use in it.

And then one day, shortly after the fall of the Berlin Wall, I had occasion to visit the State Department, and particularly those who had served on the Soviet desk, and realized as I watched them all turning to the left three times and kind of throwing their heads around that they had all committed overlearning and I then understood their problem and this was really good. All right, that's the value of a liberal arts education.

Now, I have three pieces of advice for you out of my very own life experience. Ready? First, raise hell — big time. I want ya'll to get out there and raise hell about damned near everything. My word, there is a world out there that needs fixing. Get out there and get after it! Now let me tell you, no matter what you do your whole life — whether you become doctors or lawyers or beggars or thieves — whatever you wind up doing, you will be, most of you, citizens of this country your entire life. That is a second job and it's a job that requires real responsibility.

We are at a time in our national life where the political system is pretty frankly corrupt. I know that many of you despise organized politics. You're young and idealistic and entitled to do that. But the corruption can be fixed and the heritage is too important to be let go. We are all of us collectively the heirs to the most magnificent political tradition any people has ever received. "We hold these truths to be self-evident, that all men [and women] are created equal, that they are endowed by their Creator with certain unalienable Rights, that among these are Life, Liberty and the pursuit of Happiness. That to secure these rights, Governments are instituted among Men, deriving their just powers from the consent of the governed,— That whenever any Form of Government becomes destructive of these ends, it is the Right of the People to alter or abolish it . . ."

Those principles are so profoundly revolutionary that they still echo with great force around the world after more than two hundred years. There are people today who are dying for the chance to live under those principles. They died in South Africa. They died at Tiananmen Square. They are dying today in Myanmar. And in this country we are in some danger of throwing away that entire legacy out of boredom, and cynicism, and inanition. And I constantly hear people say, "Well, I really just don't care much for politics"; "Ah well, they're all crooks, there's nothing I can do." People have a million reasons for not getting involved. The thing is, you can't back out of it, it's not your choice. You can't look at politics in this country as though it were a television program, or a picture on a wall that you could stand back and look at and decide whether or not you liked it.

Your entire life — the warp and woof of your life — is going to be bounded by political decisions made in city halls and state capitals and the White House, and the Capitol in Washington: How deep you will be buried when you die, the qualifications of the people who prescribe your eyeglasses, whether or not the dye you use on your hair will cause cancer. All of those, and many, many more things that touch your life every day in a thousand ways. Whether or not your car is safe when you get into it, all of these things are affected by government. You are involved, whether you like the picture or not. And if you don't like it, you really have an obligation to change it.

Let me point out a couple of great pieces of news about raising hell. This leads me (having impressed you with the importance of raising hell) to my second piece of advice, which is — and I'm really serious about this — you *must* have fun. You must work at having fun. Let me tell you, you can't put it off. You've gotta have fun while you're fighting to fix the world, because first of all, we don't always win, so it might get to be all the fun you'll ever have, and second of all, it's a better way to live. If you don't have fun while you're fighting to make a better world, what's gonna happen is you're gonna get tired and bitter and cynical and burnt out and just wind up a complete waste to everybody. So just put fun on your list.

In Texas, the peculiar place from which I come, we find that imagination and beer are useful.

A few years back, the state legislature in Texas took a fit of communism and declared Martin Luther King, Jr.'s birthday a state holiday. Now don't worry, it was a package deal; we kept Confederate Heroes day. Nevertheless, we now honor Dr. King's birthday as a state holiday and as y'all can imagine, it upset the Ku Klux Klan. And the Klan announced that it was coming to Austin to have a big march and a rally to protest this terrible thing. Now, it's always awful (I didn't realize civilized people in other parts of the world don't have this problem), it's always a real pain in the butt when the Kluckers come to march. It upsets the black citizens, it upsets the Jewish citizens. Skinhead kids turn out to cheer for them, people get in fist fights on the sidewalk, and everybody's mad at everybody for a good six months. And it is one's bounded duty as a good American citizen, as a civil libertarian, a believer in the Constitution and the principle of free speech, to stand up for the right of these blue-bellied nincompoops to spew whatever vicious dribble they want to. It says so right there in the First Amendment. And I will tell you that this is a stand that will make you about as popular as a whore trying to get into the SMU School of Theology. It is not gonna improve your standing with the neighbors, take my word for it.

So, a group of us dispirited civil libertarians, faced with the prospect of a Klan march, gathered over a pitcher of beer down at the Zona Rosa bar in Austin and came up with what we thought was a better plan. Now, we don't have enough Kluckers right there in Austin to have a good march. They had to be bussed in from Waco and Vidor. They got off the buses wearing their little pointy hats on their little pointy heads and commenced to march up Congress Avenue towards the capitol. They were greeted by several thousand citizens of Austin who mooned them as they marched. It made a very nice effect; it was kind of like a wave at a baseball stadium.

Not a tactic I would recommend for Minnesota in wintertime, but once again you should consider that when you are out trying to improve the world, there is no earthly reason for you not to have fun doing it. And you've got to work at that, you've got to concentrate on that. I want to pass on a quote from a wonderful fellow, Joe Rauh, who died a few years ago. He was a great American freedom fighter. He was one of the lawyers who stood up and defended people during the McCarthy era — another time of fear — the fear of the terrible threat of Communism in those days, terrorism today, that made people so afraid that they tried to make themselves safer by making themselves less free. And the funny thing is, when you make yourself less free, you're not safer, you're just less free. There is no connection. But that is an instinct that shows up repeatedly in American life, and we're going through another such episode.

So, Mr. Rauh would have been a great guy to have freedom fighting with us today. Fought during the McCarthy era, during the early days of the Civil Rights movement when it was unclear that we were going to have any kind of success there. It was always hot, and we were always scared. Rauh used to come get people out of jail and deal with authorities. And he fought on the side of the right and the good most of his life, and toward the end, one of these big national organizations was fixing to lay one of these lifetime freedom-fighter awards on him, and Joe was sick in the hospital, and asked a friend of his to go down to Philadelphia to collect the award for him. Friend went to see him in hospital, said, "Joe, what do you want me to tell these folks when I pick up the award?" He's looking at Joe lying there sick as a dog, and thinking about his life, all the struggles, all the hard times, you know, trying to fight for social justice, and racial justice, and trying to deliver on the promise of "liberty and justice for all" and all the hard battles, and all the hard work, and Joe looked up at him and said, "Oh, tell them how much fun it was. Tell them how much fun it was." Now think about it. Y'all get down toward the end of your road, I want you all to be able to turn around and tell the young people who come behind you, and believe me, if you're a woman you are going to go through some special tests, that you just had a hell of a lotta fun raising hell.

Now, my third piece of advice today — I know you would remember to do it anyway, but I think it is real important — I want y'all to thank your moms and your dads and your stepmoms and stepdads, and aunts and uncles, and everybody who helps get you through.

Have wonderful lives, go forth unafraid.

Listen to Your Heart

Thomas L. Friedman

THOMAS L. FRIEDMAN has won three Pulitzer Prizes for his incisive writing in the *New York Times*. He became the paper's foreign-affairs columnist in 1995 and had previously served as the chief economic correspondent in their Washington bureau, as chief White House correspondent, as Israel bureau chief, and as Beirut bureau chief. Mr. Friedman's books include the best-selling *Hot, Flat and Crowded*; *The World Is Flat*; *Longitudes and Attitudes*; *The Lexus and the Olive Tree*; and *From Beirut to Jerusalem*, which won the National Book Award for nonfiction in 1989.

Listen to Your Heart

Thomas L. Friedman

In his 2005 commencement address at Williams College, Thomas L. Friedman emphasizes the importance of "doing what you really love to do" and cultivating the "ability to learn how to learn."

I've been a journalist all my life. It's been a great ride. What I want to share with you are not the stories I've covered but some of the lessons I accidentally learned along the way about getting through life. As Yogi Berra once said, "You can see a lot by just listening," or maybe it was, "You can hear a lot just by watching." Either way, the reporter's life has allowed me to do a lot of both, and for the past few months I've been jotting down a few of the things that might be relevant advice to you.

Lesson #1 is very simple. As the writer Dan Pink noted in the *New York Times* just yesterday, it is a piece of advice that graduation speakers all over the land will be giving to graduates today, and it goes like this: Do what you love. But the reason that advice is no longer what Pink called "warm and gooey career advice" but actually a very "hard-headed'" survival strategy is because, as I like to put it, the world is getting flat.

What is flattening the world is our ability to automate more work with computers and software and to transmit that work anywhere in the world that it can be done more efficiently or cheaply thanks to the new global fiber optic network. The flatter the world gets, the more essential it is that you do what you love, because, as Pink notes, all the boring, repetitive jobs are going to be automated or outsourced in a flat world. The good jobs that will remain will be those that cannot be automated or outsourced; they will be the jobs that demand or encourage some uniquely human creative flair, passion, and imagination. In other words, jobs that can only be done by people who love what they do.

You see, when the world gets flat everyone should want to be an untouchable. Untouchables in my lexicon are people whose jobs cannot be outsourced or automated. They cannot be shipped to India or done by a machine. So who are the untouchables? Well, first they are people who are really special — Michael Jordan or Barbra Streisand. Their talents can never be automated or outsourced. Second are people who are really specialized — brain surgeons, designers, consultants, or artists.

Third are people who are anchored and whose jobs have to be done in a specific location — from nurses to hairdressers to chefs — and lastly, and this is going to apply to many of us, people who are really adaptable — people who can change with changing times and changing industries.

There is a much better chance that you will make yourself special, specialized, or adaptable, a much better chance that you will bring that something extra, what Dan Pink called "a sense of curiosity, aesthetics, and joyfulness" to your work, if you do what you love and love what you do.

I learned that quite by accident by becoming a journalist. It all started when I was in tenth grade. First, I took a journalism class from a legendary teacher at my high school, named Hattie Steinberg, who had more influence on me than any adult other than my parents. Under Hattie's inspiration, journalism just grabbed my imagination. Hattie was a single woman nearing sixty years old by the time I had her as a teacher. She was the polar opposite of cool. But she sure got us all excited about writing, and we hung around her classroom like it was the malt shop and she was the disc jockey "Wolfman Jack." To this day, her tenth-grade journalism class in Room 313 was the only journalism class I have ever taken. The other thing that happened to me in tenth grade, though, was that my parents took me to Israel over the Christmas break. And from that moment on, I fell in love with the Middle East. One of the first articles I ever published in my Minnesota high school paper was in tenth grade, in 1969. It was an interview with an Israeli general who had been a major figure in the '67 war. He had come to give a lecture at the University of Minnesota; his name was Ariel Sharon. Little did I know how many times our paths would cross in the years to come.

Anyway, by the time tenth grade was over, I still wasn't quite sure what career I wanted, but I sure knew what I loved: I loved journalism and I loved the Middle East. Now, growing up in Minnesota at that time, in a middle-class household, I never thought about going away to college. Like all my friends, I enrolled at the University of Minnesota. But unlike my friends, I decided to major in Arabic and Middle Eastern studies. There were not a lot of kids at the University of Minnesota studying Arabic back then. Norwegian, yes; Swedish, yes; Arabic, no. But I loved it; my parents didn't mind; they could see I enjoyed it. But if I had a dime for every time one of my parents' friends said to me, "Say Tom, your Dad says you're studying Arabic; what are you going to do with that?" Well, frankly, it beat the heck out of me. But this was what I loved and it just seemed that that was what college was for.

I eventually graduated from Brandeis with a degree in

Mediterranean studies and went on to graduate school at Oxford. During my first year in England — this was 1975 — I was walking down the street with my then-girlfriend and now-wife, Ann, and I noticed a front-page headline from the *Evening Standard* tabloid. It said, "President Carter to Jews: If Elected I Promise to Fire Dr. K." I thought, "Isn't that interesting?" Jimmy Carter is running against Gerald Ford for president, and in order to get elected, he's trying to win Jewish votes by promising to fire the first-ever Jewish Secretary of State. I thought about how odd that was and what might be behind it. And for some reason, I went back to my dorm room in London and wrote a short essay about it. No one asked me to, I just did it. Well, my then-girlfriend, now-wife's family knew the editorial-page editor of the *Des Moines Register*, and my then-girlfriend, now-wife brought the article over to him when she was home for spring break. He liked it, printed it, and paid me fifty dollars for it. And I thought that was the coolest thing in the whole world. I was walking down the street, I had an idea, I wrote it down, and someone gave me fifty dollars. I've been hooked ever since. A journalist was born and I never looked back.

So whatever you plan to do, whether you plan to travel the world next year, go to graduate school, join the workforce, or take some time off to think, don't just listen to your head.

Listen to your heart. It's the best career counselor there is. Do what you really love to do and if you don't know quite what that is yet, well, keep searching, because if you find it, you'll bring that something extra to your work that will help ensure you will not be automated or outsourced. It will help make you an untouchable radiologist, an untouchable engineer, or an untouchable teacher.

Indeed, let me close this point with a toned-down version of a poem that was written by the slam poet Taylor Mali. A friend sent it to my wife, who's a schoolteacher. It is called: "What Teachers Make." It contains some wisdom that I think belongs in every graduation speech. It goes like this: "The dinner guests were sitting around the table discussing life. One man, a CEO, decided to explain the problem with education. He argued this way. 'What's a kid going to learn from someone who decided his best option in life was to become a teacher? You know, it's true what they say about teachers: Those who can do, do; those who can't do, teach.' To corroborate his statement he said to another guest, 'Hey, Susan, you're a teacher. Be honest, what do you make?'

"Susan, who had a reputation for honesty and frankness, replied, 'You want to know what I make? I make kids work harder than they ever thought they could and I can make kids sit through forty minutes of study hall in absolute silence. I can make a C-plus feel like the Congressional Medal of Honor and an A feel like a slap in the face if the student didn't do his or her very best.' Susan continued, 'I can make parents tremble when I call home or feel almost like they won the lottery when I tell them how well their child is progressing.' Gaining speed, she went on: 'You want to know what I make? I make kids wonder, I make them question, I make them criticize, I make them apologize and mean it, I make them write and I make them read, read, read. I make them show all their work in math and hide it all on their final drafts in English.' Susan then stopped and cleared her throat. 'I make them understand that if you have the brains, then follow your heart. And if someone ever tries to judge you by what you make in money, you pay them no attention.' Susan then paused. 'You want to know what I make?' she said. 'I make a difference. What about you?'"

Lesson #2. The second lesson I learned from journalism is that being a good listener is one of the great keys to life. My friend and colleague, Bob Schieffer of CBS News, used to say to me, "The biggest stories I missed as a journalist happened because I was talking when I should have been listening." The ability to be a good listener is one of the most underappreciated talents a person or a country can have. People often ask me how I, an American Jew, have been able to operate in the Arab/Muslim world for twenty years, and my answer to them is always the same. The secret is to be a good listener. It has never failed me. You can get away with really disagreeing with people as long as you show them the respect of really listening to what they have to say and taking it into account when and if it makes sense. Indeed, the most important part of listening is that it is a sign of respect. It's not just what you hear by listening that is important. It is what you say by listening that is important. It's amazing how you can defuse a whole roomful of angry people by just starting your answer to a question with the phrase, "You're making a legitimate point" or "I hear what you say," and really meaning it. Never underestimate how much people just want to feel that they have been heard, and once you have given them that chance they will hear you.

I went to Saudi Arabia after 9/11 after having written a series of extremely critical columns about the Saudi regime. And I was always struck by how Saudis received me, Saudis who weren't prepped to receive me. The encounter would often go something like this: "Hi, I'm Tom Friedman." "The Tom Friedman who writes for the *New York Times*?" "Yes, that Tom Friedman." "You're here?" "Yes, I'm here." "They gave you a visa?" "Yes, I didn't come illegally." "You know, I hate everything you write. Would you come to my house for dinner so I could get some friends together to talk to you?"

If you really want to get through to people as a journalist, you first have to open their ears, and the best way to open their ears is to first open your own — show them the respect of listening, it's amazing what they will let you say after that, and it is amazing what you might learn.

Lesson #3 is that the most enduring skill you can bring to the workplace is also one of the most important skills journalists always had to bring to reporting — and that is the ability to learn how to learn. I have always thought that the greatest thing about being a reporter was that you just get to keep getting Master's degrees. Each time I took a new beat, from Beirut to Jerusalem to Diplomacy to the White House to the Treasury, I got to get the equivalent of a Master's degree in each of those subjects — just by reporting on them for an extended period.

I hope that you have learned how to learn. That too is going to be really important if you want to be an untouchable, because jobs are going to change faster and faster in a flat world. Believe me, I know. You see, about eighteen months ago I went to Bangalore, India, to do a documentary about outsourcing. We shot about sixty hours of film in ten days, and across those ten days I got progressively sicker and sicker. Because somewhere between the Indian entrepreneur who wanted to do my taxes from Bangalore, and the one who wanted to write my new software from Bangalore, and one who wanted to read my X-rays from Bangalore, and the one who wanted to trace my lost luggage on Delta airlines from Bangalore, I realized that people were doing things I could not explain or understand. I realized that my own intellectual software needed updating. I came home and told my editors I need to go on leave immediately. That is why I wrote *The World Is Flat.* I was retooling myself. None of us is immune from that.

Now, while I have been on book tour these few months talking about the flat world, several parents have come up to me and said, "Mr. Friedman, my daughter is studying Chinese, she's going to be okay, right?" As if this was going to be the new key to lifetime employment. Well, not exactly. I think it is great to study Chinese, I told them, but the enduring skill you really need in a flat world is an ability to learn how to learn. The ability to learn how to learn is what enables you to adapt and stay special or specialized. Well then, a ninth grader in St. Paul asked me, how do you learn how to learn?

"Wow," I said to him, "that's a really good question." I told him that I think the best way to learn how to learn is to go around and ask all your friends who are the best teachers in your school and then just take their classes, whether it is Greek Mythology or Physics. Because I think probably the best way to learn how to learn is to love learning. When I think back on my favorite teachers, I am not sure I remember much anymore of what they taught me, but I sure remember enjoying learning it.

Lesson #4 is: Don't get carried away with the gadgets. I started as a reporter in Beirut working on an Adler manual typewriter. I can tell you that the stories I wrote for the *New York Times* on that manual typewriter are still some of my favorites. In this age of laptops and PDAs, the Internet and Google, mp3s and iPods, remember one thing: all these tools might make you smarter, but they sure won't make you smart, they might extend your reach, but they will never tell you what to say to your neighbor over the fence, or how to comfort a friend in need, or how to write a lead that sings, or how to imagine a breakthrough in science or literature. You cannot download passion, imagination, zest, and creativity — all that stuff that will make you untouchable. You have to upload it, the old-fashioned way, under the olive tree, with reading, writing and arithmetic, travel, study, reflection, museum visits, and human interaction.

Look, no one is more interested in technology than I am, but the rumor is true: I was the last person in my family and on my block to get a mobile phone, and I still only use it for outgoing calls. Otherwise, as my daughters will tell you, I never keep it on. And don't leave me a message, because I still don't know how to retrieve them and I have no intention of learning. Because I can't concentrate if people are constantly pinging me. You may also have noticed, I do not put my email address on my column. Unless readers go through all the trouble to call the paper to get my Web address, if they want to communicate with me, they have to sit down and write me a letter. That is mail without an "e." And yes, I only converted to Microsoft Word when I started my latest book a year ago and that is because XyWrite, the Stone Age writing program I have been using since the 1980s, just couldn't interface anymore with my new laptop. I am not a Luddite, per se, but I am a deliberately late adopter. I prefer to keep my tools simple, so I focus as much of my energy on the listening, writing, and problem solving — not on the gadgets. That is also why if I had one fervent wish it would be that every modem sold in America would come with a warning label from the surgeon general, and that warning would simply say: "Judgment Not Included."

Lesson #5 is this: Always remember, there is a difference between skepticism and cynicism. Too many journalists, and too many of our politicians, have lost sight of that boundary line. I learned that lesson very early in my career. In 1982, I was working in the Business section of the *Times* and was befriended by a young editor there named Nathaniel Nash. Nathaniel was a gentle soul and a born-again Christian. He liked to come by and talk to me about Israel and the Holy Land. In April 1982, the *Times* assigned me to cover the Lebanese civil war, and at my office goodbye party Nathaniel whispered to me: "I'm going to pray for your safety." I never forgot that. I always considered his prayers my good luck charm, and when I walked out of Beirut in one piece three years later, one of the first things I did was thank Nathaniel for keeping watch over me. He liked that a lot.

I only wish I could have returned the favor. You see, a few years later Nathaniel gave up editing and became a reporter himself, first in Argentina and then later as the *Times* business reporter in Europe, based in Germany. Nathaniel was a wonderful reporter, who was one of the most uncynical people I ever knew. Indeed, the book on Nathaniel as a reporter was that he was too nice. His colleagues always doubted that anyone that nice could ever succeed in journalism, but somehow he triumphed over this handicap and went from one successful assignment to another. It was because Nathaniel intuitively understood that there was a big difference between skepticism and cynicism. Skepticism is about asking questions, being dubious, being wary, not being gullible, but always being open to being persuaded of a new fact or angle. Cynicism is about already having the answers — or thinking you do — answers about a person or an event. The skeptic says, "I don't think that's true; I'm going to check it out." The cynic says, "I know that's not true. It couldn't be. I'm going to slam him." Nathaniel always honored that line.

Unfortunately, Nathaniel Nash, at age forty-four, was the sole American reporter traveling on U.S. Commerce Secretary Ron Brown's airplane when it crashed into a Croatian hillside in 1996. Always remember, real journalists are not those loud-mouth talking heads you see on cable television. Real journalists are reporters, like Nathaniel Nash, who go off to uncomfortable and often dangerous places like Croatia and get on a military plane to chase after a visiting dignitary, without giving it a second thought — all to get a few fresh quotes, maybe a scoop, or even just a paragraph of color that no one else had. My prayers were too late for Nathaniel, but he was such a good soul, I am certain that right now he is sitting at God's elbow — taking notes, with skepticism not cynicism. So be a skeptic, not a cynic. We have more than enough of those in our country already, and so much more creative juice comes from skepticism, not cynicism.

Lesson #6. Nathaniel's untimely death only reinforced for me the final lesson I am going to impart to you. It's very brief. It's "Call Your Mama." For me, the most searing images and stories of 9/11 were the tales of all those people who managed to use a cell phone to call their loved ones to say a last goodbye from a hijacked airplane or a burning tower. But think of the hundreds of others who never got a chance to say goodbye or a final "I love you." There was a legendary football coach at the University of Alabama named Bear Bryant and late in his career, after his mother had died, Bell South Telephone Company asked him to do a TV commercial. As best I can piece together from the news reports, the commercial was supposed to be very simple—just a little music and Coach Bryant saying in his tough coach's voice, "Have you called your Mama today?" On the day of the filming, though, when it came time for Coach Bryant to recite his simple line, he decided to ad lib something. He looked into the camera and said, "Have you called your Mama today? I sure wish I could call mine." That was how the commercial ran, and it got a huge response from audiences. My father died when I was nineteen. He never got to see me do what I love. I sure wish I could call him. My mom is eighty-six years old and lives in a home for people with dementia. She doesn't remember so well anymore, but she still remembers that my column runs twice a week. She doesn't quite remember the days, so every day she goes through the *New York Times*, and if she finds my column, she often photocopies it and passes it out to the other dementia patients in her nursing home. If you think that isn't important to me, then you don't know what is important.

Your parents love you more than you will ever know. So if you take one lesson away from this talk, take this one: Call your Mama, regularly. And your Papa. You will always be glad you did.

That about does it for me. I'm fresh out of material. I guess what I have been trying to say here can be summed up by the old adage that "happiness is a journey, not a destination." Bringing joy and passion and optimism to your work is not what you get to do when you get to the top. It is HOW you get to the top. If I have had any success as a journalist since I started thirty years ago, it's because I found a way to enjoy the journey as much as the destination. I had almost as much fun as a cub reporter doing the overnight shift at UPI, as I did traveling with Secretary of State Baker, as I do now as a columnist. Oh yes, I have had my dull moments and bad seasons — believe me, I have. But more often than not I found ways to learn from, and enjoy, some part of each job. You can't bet your whole life on some destination. You've got to make the journey work too. And that is why I leave you with some wit and wisdom attributed to Mark Twain: Always work like you don't need the money. Always fall in love like you've never been hurt. Always dance like nobody is watching. And always — always — live like it's heaven on earth.

What I Learned

David Sedaris

With sardonic wit and incisive social critiques, DAVID SEDARIS has become one of America's preeminent humor writers. The great skill with which he slices through cultural euphemisms and political correctness proves that he is a master of satire and one of the most observant writers addressing the human condition today. Mr. Sedaris is the author of *Barrel Fever* and *Holidays on Ice*, as well as collections of personal essays, *Naked, Me Talk Pretty One Day, Dress Your Family in Corduroy and Denim, When You Are Engulfed in Flames, Squirrel Seeks Chipmunk*, and *Let's Explore Diabetes with Owls.* He lives in England, and is a contributor to the *New Yorker* and the BBC.

What I Learned

DAVID SEDARIS

In his 2006 commencement address at Princeton University, David Sedaris ponders what happens when you don't pursue the "double major" your parents had been counting on you to complete.

It's been interesting to walk around campus this afternoon, as when *I* went to Princeton things were completely different. This chapel, for instance — I remember when it was just a clearing, cordoned off with sharp sticks. Prayer was compulsory back then, and you couldn't just fake it by moving your lips; you had to know the words, and really mean them. I'm dating myself, but this was before Jesus Christ. We worshipped a God named Sashatiba, who had five eyes, including one right here, on the Adam's apple. None of us ever met him, but word had it that he might appear at any moment, so we were always at the ready. *Whatever you do, don't look at his neck*, I used to tell myself.

It's funny now, but I thought about it a lot. Some people thought about it a little too much, and it really affected their academic performance. Again, I date myself, but back then we were on a pass-fail system. If you passed, you got to live, and if you failed you were burned alive on a pyre that's now the Transgender Studies Building. Following the first grading period, the air was so thick with smoke you could barely find your way across campus. There were those who said that it smelled like meat, no different from a barbecue, but I could tell the difference. I mean, really. Since when do you grill hair? Or those ugly, chunky shoes we all used to wear?

It kept you on your toes, though, I'll say that much. If I'd been burned alive because of bad grades, my parents would have killed me, especially my father, who meant well but was just a little too gung ho for my taste. He had the whole outfit: Princeton breastplate, Princeton nightcap; he even got the velvet cape with the tiger head hanging like a rucksack from between the shoulder blades. In those days, the mascot was a sabretooth, so you can imagine how silly it looked, and how painful it was to sit down. Then, there was his wagon, completely covered with decals and bumper stickers: "I hold my horses for Ivy League schools," "My son was accepted at the best university in the United States and all I got was a bill for a hundred and sixty-eight thousand dollars." On and on, which was just so . . . *wrong*.

One of the things they did back then was start you off with a modesty seminar, an eight-hour session that all the freshmen had to sit through. It might be different today, but in my time it took the form of a role-playing exercise, my classmates and I pretending to be graduates, and the teacher assuming the part of an average citizen: the soldier, the bloodletter, the whore with a heart of gold.

"Tell me, young man. Did you attend a university of higher learning?"

To anyone holding a tool or a weapon, we were trained to respond, "What? Me go to college?" If, on the other hand, the character held a degree, you were allowed to say, "Sort of," or, sometimes, "I think so."

"So where do you sort of think you went?"

And it was the next bit that you had to get just right. Inflection was everything, and it took the foreign students forever to master it.

"Where do you sort of think you went?"

And we'd say, "Umm, Princeton?"— as if it were an oral exam, and we weren't quite sure that this was the correct answer.

"Princeton, my goodness," the teacher would say. "That must have been quite something!"

You had to let him get it out, but once he started in on how brilliant and committed you must be it was time to hold up your hands, saying, "Oh, it isn't that hard to get into."

Then he'd say, "Really? But I heard — "

"Wrong," you'd tell him. "You heard wrong. It's not that great of a school."

This was the way it had to be done—you had to play it down, which wasn't easy when your dad was out there, reading your acceptance letter into a bullhorn.

I needed to temper my dad's enthusiasm a bit, and so I announced that I would be majoring in patricide. The Princeton program was very strong back then, the best in the country, but it wasn't the sort of thing your father could get too worked up about. Or, at least, most fathers wouldn't. Mine was over the moon. "Killed by a Princeton graduate!" he said. "And my own son, no less."

My mom was actually jealous. "So what's wrong with matricide?" she asked. "What, I'm not good enough to murder?"

They started bickering, so in order to make peace I promised to consider a double major.

"And how much more is that going to cost us?" they said.

Those last few months at home were pretty tough, but then I started my freshman year, and got caught up in the life of the mind. My idol-worship class was the best, but my dad didn't get it. "What the hell does that have to do with patricide?" he asked.

And I said, "*Umm. Everything?*"

He didn't understand that it's all connected, that one subject leads to another and forms a kind of chain that raises its head and nods like a cobra when you're sucking on a bong after three days of no sleep. On acid it's even wilder, and appears to eat things. But, not having gone to college, my dad had no concept of a well-rounded liberal-arts education. He thought that all my classes should be murder-related, with no lunch breaks or anything. Fortunately, it doesn't work that way.

In truth, I had no idea what I wanted to study, so for the first few years I took everything that came my way. I enjoyed pillaging and astrology, but the thing that ultimately stuck was comparative literature. There wasn't much of it to compare back then, no more than a handful of epic poems and one novel about a lady detective, but that's part of what I liked about it. The field was new, and full of possibilities, but try telling that to my parents.

"You mean you *won't* be killing us?" my mother said. "But I told everyone you were going for that double major."

Dad followed his "I'm so disappointed" speech with a lecture on career opportunities. "You're going to study literature and get a job doing *what*?" he said. "*Literaturizing*?"

We spent my entire vacation arguing; then, just before I went back to school, my father approached me in my bedroom. "Promise me you'll keep an open mind," he said. And, as he left, he slipped an engraved dagger into my book bag.

I had many fine teachers during my years at Princeton, but the one I think of most often was my fortune-telling professor — a complete hag with wild gray hair, warts the size of new potatoes, the whole nine yards. She taught us to forecast the weather up to two weeks in advance, but ask her for anything weightier and you were likely to be disappointed.

The alchemy majors wanted to know how much money they'd be making after graduation. "Just give us an approximate figure," they'd say, and the professor would shake her head and cover her crystal ball with a little cozy given to her by one of her previous classes. When it came to our futures, she drew the line, no matter how hard we begged — and, I mean, we really tried. I was as let down as the next guy, but, in retrospect, I can see that she acted in our best interests.

Look at yourself on the day that you graduated from college, then look at yourself today. I did that recently, and it was, like, "What the hell happened?"

The answer, of course, is life. What the hag chose not to foretell — and what we, in our certainty, could not have fathomed — is that stuff comes up. Weird doors open. People fall into things. Maybe the engineering whiz will wind up brewing cider, not because he has to but because he finds it challenging. Who knows? Maybe the athlete will bring peace to all nations, or the class moron will go on to become the President of the United States — though that's more likely to happen at Harvard or Yale, schools that will pretty much let in anybody.

There were those who left Princeton and soared like arrows into the bosoms of power and finance, but I was not one of them. My path was a winding one, with plenty of obstacles along the way. When school was finished, I went back home, an Ivy League graduate with four years' worth of dirty laundry and his whole life ahead of him. "What are you going to do now?" my parents asked.

And I said, "Well, I was thinking of washing some of these underpants."

That took six months. Then I moved on to the shirts.

"Now what?" my parents asked.

And, when I told them I didn't know, they lost what little patience they had left. "What kind of a community-college answer is that?" my mother said. "You went to the best school there is — how can you not know something?"

And I said, "I don't know."

In time, my father stopped wearing his Princeton gear. My mother stopped talking about my "potential," and she and my dad got themselves a brown-and-white puppy. In terms of intelligence, it was just average, but they couldn't see that at all. "Aren't you just the smartest dog in the world?" they'd ask, and the puppy would shake their hands just like I used to do.

My first alumni weekend cheered me up a bit. It was nice to know that I wasn't the only unemployed graduate in the world, but the warm feeling evaporated when I got back home and saw that my parents had given the dog my bedroom. In place of the Princeton pennant they'd bought for my first birthday was a banner reading, "Westminster or bust."

I could see which way the wind was blowing, and so I left, and moved to the city, where a former classmate, a philosophy major, got me a job on his rag-picking crew. When the industry moved overseas — this the doing of *another* former classmate — I stayed put, and eventually found work skinning hides for a ratcatcher, a thin, serious man with the longest beard I had ever seen.

At night, I read and reread the handful of books I'd taken with me when I left home, and eventually, out of boredom as much as anything else, I started to write myself. It wasn't much, at first: character sketches, accounts of my day, parodies of articles in the alumni newsletter. Then, in time, I became more ambitious, and began crafting little stories about my family. I read one of them out loud to the ratcatcher, who'd never laughed at anything but roared at the description of my mother and her puppy. "My mom was just the same," he said. "I graduated from Brown, and two weeks later she was raising falcons on my top bunk!" The story about my dad defecating in his neighbor's well pleased my boss so much that he asked for a copy, and sent it to his own father.

This gave me the confidence to continue, and in time I completed an entire book, which was subsequently published. I presented a first edition to my parents, who started with the story about our neighbor's well, and then got up to close the drapes. Fifty pages later, they were boarding up the door and looking for ways to disguise themselves. Other people had loved my writing, but these two didn't get it at all. "What's wrong?" I asked.

My father adjusted his makeshift turban, and sketched a mustache on my mother's upper lip. "What's wrong?" he said. "I'll tell you what's wrong: you're killing us."

"But I thought that's what you wanted?"

"We did," my mother wept, "but not this way."

It hadn't occurred to me until that moment, but I seemed to have come full circle. What started as a dodge had inadvertently become my life's work, an irony I never could have appreciated had my extraordinary parents not put me through Princeton.

The Reach

Anna Deavere Smith

Anna Deavere Smith is an acclaimed actress and playwright whose innovative documentary plays have been nominated for Tony Awards and Pulitzer Prizes. Ms. Smith draws on extensive interviews to construct such powerful plays as *Let Me Down Easy*; *House Arrest*; *Twilight: Los Angeles, 1992;* and *Fires in the Mirror*. Though she is the sole performer in these plays, she brings to life a multitude of striking characters in them. In addition to her work on stage, she has been featured in the films *Rachel Getting Married*, *The American President*, and *Philadelphia*, and in the popular TV series *The West Wing*.

The Reach

Anna Deavere Smith

In her 2007 commencement address at Bates College, Anna Deavere Smith urges us to step out of the comfort zone of "safe," accepted identity to discover "the crossroads of ambiguity."

My few words to you are about community. That's a word that doesn't have a lot of teeth, and I think it's because when we look it up in dictionaries we see that it doesn't tell us anything about power. Certainly, if you've graduated from college somewhere you're interested in power.

The kind of future that's in front of us is going to require that we work in community and that we work in teams. "Community" will not just mean that which is closest to you, but that which you can reach. And what's so important is how long your reach is, in terms of how far will you go, either by being present or through technology. But beware, as my good friend Studs Terkel, that great radioman from Chicago, said, "We're more and more into communications, and less and less into communication!" So, just because we can reach each other through technology, doesn't mean we've really connected.

Sometimes, working in community and teams is going to call for more stamina than you might think you have. When I think of stamina, I think about Brent Williams, a bull rider whom I met in Idaho, who talked about hanging on the bull even if you're riding upside-down. You're going to hang onto that bull until your head hits the dirt.

The reason that community and reach and stamina are so important now is that many of us have been educated to celebrate our own identities, to celebrate that which we understand because that's what we came from. I like to think about us existing in what I call "safe houses of identity." There's the black woman's house, the white woman's house, the educated person's house, the illiterate person's house. I suggest to you that you come out of your safe houses of identity, even as your education may have rightfully nurtured you in the archives of those identities. Come out of that into a space that I call "the crossroads of ambiguity," where there is no house, where it is not safe.

I've talked to my students about resilience, about what the bull rider is trying to teach us, where there is no roof and where you might make a brand-new house with someone who doesn't speak a language that you speak. Living this way is going to call for a greater sense of mobility, and in that "mobileness" also keeping a sense of kindness, of music, of humor, and, mostly, never to think you know where you are.

When I arrived at a Hilton the other day — and I've seen more Hilton hotels than you want to know about — I didn't even bother opening the curtains. I was sure I would look at a parking lot or another building. Right before I went to bed, I thought that I better open the curtains, to make sure I'd wake up. When I woke up, I saw an extraordinary waterfall. And so, even at the moment we think we know something, if we stop to open the curtain, to open our eyes, to open our hearts in another way, there just might be that waterfall. And that waterfall might just lead us to a new thought or a new spirit.

Be strong, be new, be you. The "be new" is even more important than the "be you."

You Are Not Alone

Karen Tse

KAREN TSE founded International Bridges to Justice in 2000 to promote systemic global change in the administration of criminal justice. A former public defender, she moved to Cambodia in 1994 to train the country's first core group of public defenders and subsequently served as a United Nations Judicial Mentor. Under the auspices of the UN, she trained judges and prosecutors, and established the first arraignment court in Cambodia. She negotiated groundbreaking measures in judicial reform with the Chinese, Vietnamese, and Cambodian governments. Under her leadership, IBJ has expanded its programming to include Rwanda, Burundi, Zimbabwe, and India. In addition to the Defenders Resource Centers in those countries, IBJ also awarded fifty-five innovative JusticeMakers fellows in thirty-seven countries. In 2010, IBJ launched the Justice Training Center in Singapore. A graduate of UCLA Law School and Harvard Divinity School, Ms. Tse was named by *U.S. News & World Report* as one of America's Best Leaders in 2007. She was the recipient of the 2008 Harvard Divinity School's First Decade Award, and the 2008 American Bar Association's International Human Rights Award. She also received the 2009 Gleitsman International Award at the Harvard Kennedy School of Government.

You Are Not Alone

Karen Tse

In her 2007 commencement address at Scripps College, Karen Tse describes how life has taught her a powerful truth: that as we begin to change the world, we, ourselves, "are transformed as well."

I want to start with a poem. The author is anonymous.

May we be reminded here of our highest aspirations,
and inspired to bring our gifts of love and service
to the altar of humanity.

May we know once again that we are not isolated beings
but connected, in mystery and miracle,
to the universe, to this community, and to each other.

As I walk through my personal journey, I'm hoping I can share a piece of what I've learned, and to invite you on this journey with me, and with the courageous human rights defenders throughout the world, who are looking to end torture in the twenty-first century.

The first thing I want to say to anyone who's on their own journey is, don't worry about a thing.

I remember sitting at my commencement when I graduated from college and feeling some excitement, and also a lot of apprehension. Apprehension because I really didn't know what was ahead. I wasn't sure that my parents or other people would agree with what I was going to do. I wasn't sure that I was able to make it, or that I would make the right decisions. Only within the last ten years, I've started to realize that really, you shouldn't worry about a thing, because there are chapters in your life. And there's an ability to wake up to life, and realize that we can learn to tolerate ambiguity. There's supposed to be a number of pieces to the heroic journey. The first piece is receiving the call to leave the known. That's where you're in a place, and you're comfortable, and then you get a call to adventure. You're very excited at first when you get that call, you're going to go out and do it.

The second piece is the act of leaving the known, leaving something that you already know, and that can be a very frightening process. You might think, "Maybe I don't want to go." But in some cases, you really have no choice.

The third piece is that there's always chaos before creation. That's a point where you could get depressed, it could be difficult, you may start or not start back and forth, but there's some chaos involved in that. So, if you're in a place of chaos, that's good, because then you're about to create.

The fourth piece is the courageous act where you actually decide, *Okay, I'm going to go for it. It's kind of scary, chaos before creation, but I'm going for it.* You do the courageous act, and then you find the treasure. After finding the treasure, you're able to bring the gift back to the world. Now, this heroic journey, which all of us are called into (and we go through many heroic journeys, throughout every point of our lives), is really of a cyclical nature. So you may be in one place, but you should always remember that wherever you are, you're going to keep going through these steps, and it will happen over and over in your life.

I've also seen that when I was sitting in one place, thinking I have to decide between divinity school, law school, or going on a Watson Fellowship, or thinking that I have to make a decision about where am I going to go, or if I should just do nothing — and that I have to make the right decision now, because it matters, but it doesn't really matter. Because in the end, you'll live through chapter three of your life. And then you'll hit chapter five of your life, and you'll think, "Gee, chapter five has nothing to do with chapter three," but in chapter seven, all of a sudden, they connect back together. This is the piece that we have to remember: That it's not just about the local story, what we see now, but there's the greater picture, there's something out there that is maybe more than we can understand.

Now, all of us have dreams. Who amongst us hasn't had wonderful dreams that we have fulfilled, but also shattered dreams? All of us have had shattered dreams. But as we put everything together in the mosaic of our lives, we begin to understand that it isn't only the local piece, the small piece, that we have to focus on, but a bigger piece as well. I've also come to understand and realize that it is important for each and every one of us to declare ourselves a contribution to this world, in whatever form that is. There are many times in my life where I have wondered about that, and I thought, should I really say anything? I remember this happening when I was a Scripps student, and when I was in divinity school, and law school as well. I was absolutely timid, and I never wanted to raise my hand, so in every class, I'd sit there and say to myself, "Okay, okay, okay. Raise your hand, raise your hand," but I could never bring myself to do it. Every time it was a challenge. It's still a challenge for me in many ways.

One lesson that I learned really came to me through a four-year-old that I met some years ago in Cambodia. His name was Vishna. He was in Cambodia, born in the prison of Kandal Province. He was born there because his mother was pregnant at the time that she was imprisoned. Now Vishna had special privileges. Even the guards said, "Well, he's a baby so let's be nice to him," and as he grew up, they let him slip in and out of the bars. When I met him, though, he was getting older and could no longer get through the bottom rungs of the prison bars. But he could climb up to the third bar, which was slightly bigger, then slowly turn his head to the side and then find a way to barely pass through the bars to the other side. Vishna was born with very little material comfort. Someone could say, "What does he have to contribute to the prison, to the world?" but the amazing thing to me about Vishna was that he was a boy with an absolutely strong sense of his own heroic journey, his own heroic value, and that there was something that he could do. And I think that he thought in his own mind, "I'm one, maybe I'm only one. I can't do everything, but I can do something, so I'm going to do what I can do."

So every day, Vishna would come out of the prison and come down the third, the second, the first rungs of the bars, and he would run out and grab my little pinkie, and he would want me to take him to each of the prison cells. Now, he didn't always make it through the 153 cells, but he'd want me to pick him up so he could poke his little finger through the bars. There were a lot of dark cells — and he would stick his head down and put his fingers through, looking into these dark cells. And to many of the people in the prison, he was their greatest joy. He was their sunshine.

What I've learned from Vishna is that this is absolutely true of each of us in this world, that we each have something to offer. Each of us is gifted in a very particular way. It's our own creative genius that is a gift to the world, and it is really about how we decide to unleash it and give it to the world — and to accept in ourselves that none of us are perfect. So you may have a strength, you may have a weakness, but you can embrace that piece of who you are and give of yourself in the best way possible to transform the world.

In this day and age, I firmly believe that we are on the edge of a human rights revolution, that there's never before been a time in history that we could really do what we can do now for human rights. Only in the last decade, countries throughout the world have passed new laws. The laws say you have a right to a lawyer, you have a right not to be tortured, but as we all know, people are still tortured everywhere in the world on a daily basis. Now, when I graduated from Scripps, most countries did not have these laws, and so what we could do was write letters protesting the government, saying this is what the situation is, let this political prisoner out. But in 1994, I walked into a prison in Cambodia, and I met a twelve-year-old boy who had been tortured and was denied access to counsel. As I looked into his eyes, I realized that, for all the hundreds of letters that I had written for political prisoners, I would never have written a letter for this boy because he wasn't an important political prisoner who had done anything important for anyone. He was a twelve-year-old boy who had stolen a bicycle. I hit upon a life-transforming realization.

Perhaps ten years ago, there might have been precious little that we could have done for this boy. Since that time, however, governments throughout the world, including Cambodia, have passed new laws outlawing torture and providing citizens with basic rights, including their right to a defender. It was precisely because this boy was not a political prisoner, someone the government had any interest in, that he could easily have been the beneficiary of focused international attention. Citizens like him were unimportant to the government, and the denial of their basic rights had less to do with the policy that was current and more to do with vestiges of an old legal system that formerly tolerated and even condoned this denial of rights.

In his face, I recognized the thousands like him who would be the direct beneficiaries of a functioning criminal justice system with a standard of basic human rights. By helping these countries to implement their own domestic laws consistent with human rights principles and helping to safeguard prisoner rights, we have the opportunity to drastically improve and perhaps even save the lives of everyday citizens.

I believe that if each of us were to make this commitment, this worldwide commitment to helping all of these countries — right now there are still 130 countries in the world that still practice torture, and in ninety-three of these countries the laws safeguarding the rights of the accused exist on the books — we can bring hope to the darkest corners of the world. The governments are open to having us come in and help them. It is really a new day and age. There was a time, when I graduated from Scripps twenty-one years ago, that we really couldn't go in because the governments said, "No way, you cannot go in." But this is a time when we can come from a different place, we can come from a place of love, we can say, "Can we work together?"

Now, I will admit that at the time, twenty-one years ago, I was a different person in many ways than I am now. I felt that we should only be angry and we should only protest. I now believe that there is a time and a place for protest. I realized something very profound a number of years ago when I was working in the prisons of Cambodia, and working with the police officers. At the time, I was training police officers, who tortured a number of people, and I couldn't really figure out what we should do because they were continuing to torture people. I remember going to my boss, because I worked for the United Nations, and I said, "What should I do? What should I do here? They want to keep torturing." And my boss said, "Tell them what the laws are; it will be okay." And finally I went to a sister at Missionaries of Charity. Her name was Sister Rose and she was from India. I said, "Sister Rose, what should I do here?" And she gave me a very important piece of advice that has changed completely the way that I perceive human rights. She said, "You know, Karen, whatever you do, you should look for the Christ, you should look for the Buddha, in each person that you work with." She really believed in the power of transformative love, and through that power, people would shift and be changed. I took her advice, and I was amazed at the change within the guards, within the prisons. They let me in, they took out all the dark cells, they began to shift their own perspective. And I began to see that there was a strength and a power that went beyond the logical, that went beyond just the laws.

It's true that with great power comes great responsibility, and as you bring your knowledge forward on your journey, you must also bring your love forward. You must bring your whole heart forward. You must bring the pieces of who you are, even when it's difficult. I say that, and I think to myself,

I've got at least 50 percent of people hearing this laughing at me right now, but I really believe that as we transform the world, it's not only the situation that's changed, but we, ourselves, who are transformed as well.

I remember being amazed one day in Vietnam as I walked and saw a man who was working with street children. And these were the street children who you'd walk past in an airport, and you wouldn't want to be around them because they would probably be pickpocketing you or doing something strange. But I saw him, and he had this great safe house where the kids were supporting each other and singing songs, and they were all street kids who had been in and out of prison. I said to him, "This is amazing, what you've done with the kids. Tell me how you started, what did you do?" And he said, "Okay, I'll tell you," because I was in great admiration of him. He said, "You know, a number of years ago, I was a heroin addict myself, and one day, I came out of prison, and I saw the police picking up these boys for stealing eggs. And I shook my head and I said, 'You know what, it might be okay that I'm in prison, but these children should not be in prison,' and at that moment, I turned, and I said to some of my friends, 'Okay, I'm going to take off my hat, and I'm going to pass the hat. We're going to do something for these children.'"

And so he said, "I passed the hat, we got a little bit of money, wasn't much, but we decided, we'd do something." What they decided to do was that on every Sunday they would gather the children in a park, and for that one day, the children would be children, meaning they'd play jump rope, and do different fun things. It was really an amazing process. After a number of years, this man and others developed safe houses and began to transform the system for these children. What the man said to me was this: "You know, I thought that I was doing it for the children, but when I was doing it for the children, I realized that I, myself, was transformed by the process."

As you go forward in your daily life, be alive to the mystery and adventure of life, know that you have the opportunity for birth and rebirth every day, and that in the process of giving to the greater world, you will be transformed too. It won't always be an easy heroic journey for you, and it may be something that's sometimes difficult. It's one thing to be happy and joyful when things are going right, but when things are going wrong, that is the most important time for you to step forward with courage and realize that courage is also the ability to have radical self-affirmation in light of whatever else is going on in your life, to believe that you'll get through to the next level.

In China, we have a number of Chinese defenders who often feel vulnerable themselves. There have been cases where they're standing up for the rights of clients who might be tortured, and at times at the end of the trial, the judge or the prosecutor will point to them and say, "You yourself have obstructed justice." They will order the lawyers handcuffed, and the lawyers will be brought to jail and they'll be beaten until they're bloody. But the lawyers have begun to band together and be strong for each other. And one poem that we always read with them is by Wayne Arnason. It is:

Take courage, friends
The road is often long
The path is never clear
The stakes are very high
But deep down there is another truth
You are not alone.

Thank you for joining me on this journey. I hope you, too, will open your heart to the many human rights defenders throughout the world. Strengthen them with your courage. Give courage and strength to others in your life in the years to come, and may you always be blessed.

Speaking Freely

Ian McEwan

IAN McEWAN is the author of fourteen novels and two collections of stories. His first published work, a collection of short stories, *First Love, Last Rites,* won the Somerset Maugham Award. His novels include *The Child in Time,* which won the 1987 Whitbread Novel of the Year Award, *The Cement Garden, Enduring Love, Amsterdam*, which won the 1998 Booker Prize, *Atonement, Saturday, On Chesil Beach, Solar,* and *Sweet Tooth*. His most recent novel is *The Children Act.*

Speaking Freely

Ian McEwan

In his 2015 commencement address at Dickinson College, Ian McEwan takes a thought-provoking look at how "freedom of expression sustains all the other freedoms we enjoy" and that "without free speech, democracy is a sham."

My most sincere congratulations to all the graduates here. You made it through. You have a degree from a truly excellent institution. A lot of reading, writing, lying in bed (thinking, of course). And now you stand on one of life's various summits. As you know, there's only one way off a summit — but that's another story. Don't be taken in by those who tell you that life is short. It's inordinately long. I was into my twenties when my mother astonished me by saying wistfully, "I'd give anything to be forty-five again." Forty-five sounded like old age to me then. Now I see what she meant. Most of you have more than twenty years before you peak. Barring all-out nuclear war or a catastrophic meteor collision, a substantial minority of you will get a toe in the door of the next century — a very wrinkled, arthritic toe, but the same toe you're wearing now. You have a lot of years in the bank – but don't worry, I'm not here to tell you how to spend them.

Instead, I would like to share a few thoughts with you about free speech (and speech here includes writing and reading, listening and thinking) — free speech — the life blood, the essential condition of the liberal education you've just received. Let's begin on a positive note: there is likely more free speech, free thought, free enquiry on earth now than at any previous moment in recorded history (even taking into account the golden age of the so-called 'pagan' philosophers). And you've come of age in a country where the enshrinement of free speech in the First Amendment is not an empty phrase, as it is in many constitutions, but a living reality.

But free speech was, it is and always will be, under attack — from the political right, the left, the centre. It will come from under your feet, from the extremes of religion as well as from unreligious ideologies. It's never convenient, especially for entrenched power, to have a lot of free speech flying around.

The words associated with Voltaire (more likely, his sentiments but not his actual phrasing) remain crucial and should never be forgotten: I disapprove of what you say, but I will defend to the death your right to say it. It's only rarely appropriate to suppress the speech of those you disagree with. As my late friend Christopher Hitchens used to say, when you meet a flat-earther or a creationist, it can be useful to be made to remember just why you think the earth is round or whether you're capable of making the case for natural selection. For that reason, it's a poor principle, adopted in some civilised countries, to imprison the deniers of the Holocaust or the Armenian massacres, however contemptible they might be.

It's worth remembering this: freedom of expression sustains all the other freedoms we enjoy. Without free speech, democracy is a sham. Every freedom we possess or wish to possess (of habeas corpus and due process, of universal franchise and of assembly, union representation, sexual equality, of sexual preference, of the rights of children, of animals — the list goes on) has had to be freely thought and talked and written into existence. No single individual can generate these rights alone. The process is cumulative. It was a historical context of relative freedom of speech that made possible the work of those who were determined to extend that liberty. John Milton, Tom Paine, Mary Wollstonecraft, George Washington, Thomas Jefferson, John Stuart Mill, Oliver Wendell

Holmes — the roll call is long and honourable — and that is why an education in the liberal arts is so vital to the culture you are about to contribute to.

Take a long journey from these shores as I'm sure many of you will, and you will find the condition of free expression to be desperate. Across almost the entire Middle East, free thought can bring punishment or death, from governments or from street mobs or motivated individuals. The same is true in Bangladesh, Pakistan, across great swathes of Africa. These past years the public space for free thought in Russia has been shrinking. In China, state monitoring of free expression is on an industrial scale. To censor daily the Internet alone, the Chinese government employs as many as fifty thousand bureaucrats — a level of thought repression unprecedented in human history.

Paradoxically, it's all the more important to be vigilant for free expression wherever it flourishes. And nowhere has it been more jealously guarded than under the First Amendment of the U.S. Constitution. Which is why it has been so puzzling lately, when we saw scores of American writers publicly disassociating themselves from a PEN gala to honour the murdered journalists of the French satirical magazine, *Charlie Hebdo*. American PEN exists to defend and promote free speech. What a disappointment that so many American authors could not stand with courageous fellow writers and artists at a time of tragedy. The magazine has been scathing about racism. It's also scathing about organised religion and politicians and it might not be to your taste — but that's when you should remember your Voltaire.

Hebdo's offices were fire-bombed in 2011, and the journalists kept going. They received constant death threats — and they kept going. In January nine colleagues were murdered, gunned down, in their office — the editorial staff kept going and within days they had produced an edition whose cover forgave their attackers. Tout est pardonné, all is forgiven. All this, when in the U.S. and U.K. one threatening phone call can be enough to stop a major publishing house in its tracks.

The attack on *Charlie Hebdo* came from religious fanatics whose allegiances became clear when one of the accomplices made her way from France, through Turkey to ISIS in Syria. Remember, this is a form of fanaticism whose victims, across Africa and the Middle East, are mostly Muslims — Muslim gays and feminists, Muslim reformists, bloggers, human rights activists, dissidents, apostates, novelists, and ordinary citizens, including children, murdered in or kidnapped from their schools.

There's a phenomenon in intellectual life that I call bi-polar thinking. Let's not side with *Charlie Hebdo* because it might seem as if we're endorsing George Bush's 'war on terror'. This is a suffocating form of intellectual tribalism and a poor way of thinking for yourself. As a German novelist friend wrote to me in anguish about the PEN affair — "It's the Seventies again: Let's not support the Russian dissidents, because it would get 'applause from the wrong side.'" That terrible phrase.

But note the end of the *Hebdo* affair: the gala went ahead, the surviving journalists received a thunderous and prolonged standing ovation from American PEN.

Timothy Garton Ash reminds us in a new book on free speech that "The U.S. Supreme Court has described academic freedom as a 'special concern of the First Amendment.'" Worrying too, then, is the case of Ayaan Hirsi Ali, an ex-Muslim, highly critical of Islam, too critical for some. As a victim herself, she has campaigned against female genital mutilation. She has campaigned for the rights of Muslim women. In a recent book she has argued that for Islam to live more at ease in the modern world it needs to rethink its attitudes to homosexuality, to the interpretation of the Koran as the literal word of God, to blasphemy, to punishing severely those who want to leave the religion. Contrary to what some have suggested, such arguments are neither racist nor driven by hatred. But she has received death threats. Crucially, on many American campuses she is not welcomed, and, notoriously, Brandeis withdrew its offer of an honorary degree. Islam is worthy of respect, as indeed is atheism. We want respect flowing in all directions. But religion and atheism, and all thought systems, all grand claims to truth, must be open to criticism, satire, even, sometimes, mockery. Surely, we have not forgotten the lessons of the Salman Rushdie affair.

Campus intolerance of inconvenient speakers is hardly new. Back in the sixties my own university blocked a psychologist for promoting the idea of a hereditable component to intelligence. In the seventies, the great American biologist E.O. Wilson was drowned out for suggesting a genetic element in human social behaviour. As I remember, both men were called fascists. The ideas of these men did not fit prevailing ideologies, but their views are unexceptionable today.

More broadly — the Internet has, of course, provided extraordinary possibilities for free speech. At the same time, it has taken us onto some difficult and unexpected terrain. It has led to the slow decline of local newspapers, and so removed a sceptical and knowledgeable voice from local politics.

Privacy is an essential element of free expression; the Snowden files have revealed an extraordinary and unnecessary level of email surveillance by government agencies. Another essential element of free expression is access to information; the Internet has concentrated huge power over that access into the hands of private companies like Google, Facebook, and Twitter. We need to be careful that such power is not abused. Large pharmaceutical companies have been known to withhold research information vital to the public interest. On another scale, the death of young black men in police custody could be framed as the ultimate sanction against free expression. As indeed is poverty and poor educational resources.

All these issues need the input of men and women with a liberal arts education and you, graduates, are well placed to form your own conclusions. And you may reasonably conclude that free speech is not simple. It's never an absolute. We don't give space to proselytising paedophiles, to racists (and remember, race is not identical to religion) or to those who wish to incite violence against others. Wendell Holmes's hypothetical 'shouting fire in a crowded theatre' is still relevant. But it can be a little too easy sometimes to dismiss arguments you don't like as 'hate speech' or to complain that this or that speaker makes you feel 'disrespected.' Being offended is not to be confused with a state of grace; it's the occasional price we all pay for living in an open society. Being robust is no bad thing. Either engage, with arguments — not with banishments and certainly not with guns — or, as an American Muslim teacher said recently at Friday prayers, ignore the entire matter.

In making your mind up on these issues, I hope you'll remember your time at Dickinson and the novels you may have read here. It would prompt you, I hope, in the direction of mental freedom. The novel as a literary form was born out of the Enlightenment, out of curiosity about and respect for the individual. Its traditions impel it towards pluralism, openness, a sympathetic desire to inhabit the minds of others. There is no man, woman, or child, on earth whose mind the novel cannot reconstruct. Totalitarian systems are right with regard to their narrow interests when they lock up novelists. The novel is, or can be, the ultimate expression of free speech.

I hope you'll use your fine liberal education to preserve for future generations the beautiful and precious but also awkward, sometimes inconvenient and even offensive culture of freedom of expression we have. Take with you these celebrated words of George Washington: "If the freedom of speech is taken away then, dumb and silent, we may be led like sheep to the slaughter."

We may be certain that Dickinson has not prepared you to be sheep. Good luck 2015 graduates in whatever you choose to do in life.

“Be Naked as Often as Possible”: Anthropological Advice

Genevieve Bell

GENEVIEVE BELL is a Vice President and Intel Fellow in the Corporate Strategy Office at Intel. Dr. Bell joined Intel in 1998 as a researcher in the Corporate Technology Group's People and Practices Research team — Intel's first social science oriented research team. She helped drive the company's first non-U.S. field studies to inform business group strategy and products and conducted groundbreaking work in urban Asia in the early 2000s. Prior to joining Intel, Dr. Bell was a lecturer in the Department of Anthropology at Stanford University. She has written more than twenty-five journal articles and book chapters on a range of subjects focused on the intersection of technology and society. Her book, *Telling Techno-Cultural Tales*, co-authored with Professor Paul Dourish, was published by MIT Press in 2011. Raised in Australia, Dr. Bell received her Bachelor's degree in Anthropology from Bryn Mawr College in 1990. She received her M.S. and Ph.D. in Anthropology from Stanford University in 1993 and 1998, respectively.

"Be Naked as Often as Possible": Anthropolgical Advice

Genevieve Bell

In her 2008 commencement address at UC Berkeley School of Information, Genevieve Bell illuminates the "four ways of being" that will be invaluable for experiencing the world.

Ten years ago, almost to the day, I sat in the sculpture garden at Stanford University and received my own Ph.D., in cultural anthropology. I don't remember anything the commencement speaker said. It was hot, and I was exhausted and overwhelmed and giddy. But I was lucky enough to have dear friends and family with me to mark what was, for all intents and purposes, a significant rite of passage in my life. And like many other rites of passage, everyone had an opinion about how I should be feeling and what I should do next. I don't want to add to that chorus, for I know how frustrating that can be. Instead, what I want to do is offer some very anthropological advice — the kind we give to students as they embark on their first fieldwork projects, leaving our universities and research labs for new places and new experiences.

Anthropologists, it turns out, are full of advice. What do the following statements all have in common? "The safest seat is always the one directly behind the driver." "Take 10 grams of quinine every night and keep off the women." "Walk in cheap sandshoes, the water runs out of them faster." And "Always lie to customs officials." Well, they are all pieces of advice given by anthropologists to would-be anthropologists before they set off to the field. My mother was cautioned not to drown in data and always to carry her own water. Seeking guidance before his first field trip to Papua New Guinea, one of my colleagues was told: "Be naked as often as possible." As it turns out, this is medical advice — being naked allows one to check for leeches and bugs and prevent all manner of unpleasant growths and fungal infections.

Leeches, bugs, and unpleasant medical issues are familiar things to me — I had taken quinine, and had had scabies, trachoma, and head-lice (self-imported to my head) before I was ten. I grew up in the field, in my mother's field sites in Australia. She is an anthropologist, too, and we joke in my family that anthropology is less a career and more a way of being in the world. Perhaps it is no surprise then that my earliest and most vivid memories are cultural in nature: the feel of a Balinese dance costume as I was bound into it and discovered I could no longer bend in the middle; the stories from elderly men and women who remembered what their part of Australia was like before European settlers arrived; the smoky smell of animal fat and ochre as Aboriginal women painted their country on my body; the moment when I realized that I was expected to be, as they would say at Ali-Curang, "boss for myself" — and I was only eight. Even as a child, this is what I knew anthropology to be — it changed you forever. Today, it is still those moments when the unfamiliar pierces me that I treasure: the sweet taste of freshwater fish from the Coorong served at a Ngarrinderi wake; the call to salat rising above the ceaseless sounds of Jakarta's traffic; the sight of hundreds of tiny decaying plastic Buddhas at a Pusan temple, each one representing someone's personal prayer or hope. And what distinguishes these moments from a stream of photos on Flickr or at a retro slide night is the way it felt for me to be there and how challenging it was to see the world through other people's eyes.

I am often asked how I ended up at Intel — as it seemed then an unlikely career choice for such an anthropologist. I met a man in a bar in Palo Alto. He owned a start-up and had connections at Intel. He claimed to be intrigued by what I did and concerned about my future, I took this to be a fairly standard bar ploy and went home, alone. Although I did not give him my name or number, he tracked me down to Stanford the next day and offered me a job. The rest, as they say, is history. The moral of this story is, "Don't give your number to strange men in bars — if they want to find you they will anyway."

The early days at Intel were exhausting: I had a policy of saying yes to everything and as a result, I spent a lot of time trying to explain to engineers and computer scientists why people were important and why knowing something about what they cared about could fundamentally shape the way new technology was developed. I spent seven years doing that. I did fieldwork in Asia and Europe and spent time in the homes of hundreds of different families getting a sense of what made them tick and what they cared about. It was a remarkable privilege. These days, I am the Director of User Experience within Intel's Digital Home Group. I manage an inter-disciplinary team of social scientists, interaction designers, and human factors engineers. We strive to stay ahead of Intel's technology roadmap. We use the insights gained for in-depth ethnographic and design research to help drive innovations in and around Intel platforms. And we create technology that responds to human needs, desires, and aspirations. And when I get a chance, I still do fieldwork.

Before I embarked on my very first fieldwork trip, I went to my advisor seeking guidance, something memorable and apt. After all, thirty years before, his supervisor had advised him, "Arthur, take a slow boat to China," and he did. His slow boat trip helped create the necessary break between the daily routines and regimes of life as a graduate student at Cornell, and the days of walking through rice-paddies in Taiwan interviewing elderly Han women about their fertility patterns over a lifetime. It created a moment, an interstice in which he could change gears. And I so wanted that same kind of sage advice from him. But he sent me to his wife. Drawing on prior experiences with a student detained at the Chinese border because the nature of her underwear suggested sex worker not social scientist, my supervisor's wife told me to "wear underwear appropriate for the occasion." It was his wife's guidance about underwear, and Arthur's injunction, "And remember Genevieve, show it to no one," that would be my fieldwork advice story. Given that I did fieldwork in Washington, D.C. in the mid-1990s when a glimpse of the 'wrong underwear' was nearly enough to bring down a president, in retrospect I should be more grateful.

So I won't tell you to take a slow boat to China, though it could be a marvelous thing to do, and I am going to assume that you have already learnt the necessary lessons about underwear and nakedness. What I wanted to do instead is give you the advice that I give my own students — my own cheat sheet, if you will, about how best to do fieldwork. Now, I know that the lives ahead of you are clearly not fieldwork. You will not, for instance, get a National Science Foundation grant to do your laundry and chances are you will not write papers on the basis of your experiences navigating the minutiae of taxation forms, workforce safety, or the tenure ladder. But insofar as you are embarking on a new passage from where you have been and that which is familiar will be a little less so — and your new experiences will transform you — fieldwork advice might come in handy.

I have four ways of being that I think are important for good fieldwork experiences and for life after graduate school. I think you have to be present, vulnerable, surprised, and brave.

A young woman I met in India once told me that to be Indian was to know it through the tips of your fingers — it was about how it felt to put your hand into a *biriyani*. Teaching me about India then meant feeding me. Anthropologists like to get in the middle of things this way — it is how we learn, it is why we go to the field and why we stay there and why we put such a premium on really being there, too. When I am in the field, I take the contemporary equivalent of a slow boat to China. I turn off my mobile phone, I log off the computer and the Internet. I read the local papers, I eat local food, I keep local hours, I talk to anyone who will listen, and I listen to anyone who will talk! For all of you, I hope this means you have the opportunity to know a place through your fingertips; to be intimately and persistently immersed in the places you will call home. Walk its streets if you can; know the way it smells and sounds, discover the local secrets and keep them. In so doing, I hope you can achieve a balance of online and off-line encounters with the people, spaces, and practices around you. I hope you can be fully engaged with local issues and the ways in which global ones are manifested around you. And I hope you experience moments of profound dislocation and discomfort — when things aren't familiar — because I firmly believe it is in those moments that we learn the most about ourselves and what we truly value.

Moments of being overwhelmed are, for me, another critical part of being in the field, and achieving them is another piece of advice I would offer you. One of the hardest things for most anthropologists in doing fieldwork is letting go of any sense that you know what is going on. My mother writes about the ways in which the Aboriginal women with whom she worked could not believe that a woman her age did not know how to hunt and kill iguana or track animals. In Asia, many families with whom I worked worried that I did not have a husband and went to great lengths to secure one for me. But it was a shaman in Korea who reminded me in a powerful and unexpected way that being in the field also means being vulnerable, in part because you cannot always anticipate what will happen next. We were sitting in her an-bang on white cotton-covered mattresses eating watermelon — it was summer and hot in Seoul. She had been talking about the visions she has had all her life and her mission to appropriately honor the souls of the Korean War dead she believes still haunt her country. She turned to me and said, "You are haunted too, aren't you?" And I knew she meant my grandfather who died when I was thirteen, and there, in front of one of my research assistants and several other strangers, I just cried. Tears streamed down my face and I couldn't stop them and no one in that room minded. I tell my students and my employees that if they aren't in tears, like this, at least once in the field, then they really aren't embracing the experience. And I suppose in the weeks and months ahead there are going to be moments of overwhelm-ing frustration and hopefully joy but, like my students, you have to be willing to be open to it all. Most of you have lived parts of your lives online, in ways my cohorts and those of my parents' generation could not imagine — though many of them embrace it now. But I am suggesting a different kind of openness and vulnerability. One that engages you and de-centers you, and requires you not to be at the center of attention or a social network. This kind of vulnerability, or humility, brings with it grace.

Maintain your ability to be surprised — this takes work but is another important part of how to be in the world and another piece of anthropological advice I would give you. Experiencing surprise is a really good thing as it marks the moments when we encounter the stuff that doesn't fit into our worldviews. It is when our assumptions are most clearly revealed, allowing us to move past them. I encourage my students and my employees to work on being curious, about everything. You have to willing to ask stupid questions, to look foolish, so that you can also be surprised. You have to ask, as I did once in Malaysia, "So are your dead relatives calling you then?" I had just found a replica mobile phone made of colored cardboard in a funerary goods store and I was inquiring how such things functioned. In Chinese culture, paper objects are burnt during a particular annual festival to take care of deceased relatives — fire transforms the paper objects into real objects in the afterlife. And in Malaysia the afterlife is teeming with new technology — mobile phones, flat-panel TVs, karaoke machines, laptops. And it turns out the dead are calling each other, on newly upgraded cell phones with lots of prepaid minutes. This was a wonderfully revelatory surprise and helped me rethink the ways technology fits into people's lives, both here and in the afterlife. But what will surprise look like for you? I hope it means that you can cultivate a strong sense of curiosity and an ability to ask the questions that lead to the moments of surprise. I hope it means that you can find ways to ask the 'stupid questions' about new technologies, information systems, and socio-technical practices. The questions that challenge the received wisdoms: Is social networking a good thing? Will having access to the Internet and laptops improve the lives of kids living in developing nations? Who is really on the other side of the digital divide? Do people really want to be constantly connected? I hope you can also find ways to stay curious and never to assume that you know it all, because you don't!

And last but not least, in my anthropological advice-giving, I urge you to be honest and brave. For anthropologists, this means staying true to the stories we were told in the field, and keeping the details and nuances, however inconvenient and contradictory they might be. It also means telling those stories in a way that is open and accessible. I remind my students and my employees that they have a responsibility to get it right — that when someone shares the details of their lives with you, you have a duty of care to do the right thing with that information. At Intel this means I have fought very hard to give presentations that honored the people whose homes I had visited. I learned to resist answering questions like: "What are the three key-takeaways about China?" Instead I insisted that they had to know about history, and culture, and politics and perhaps then the right answers would be clearer. It has meant, over the years, that we have haunted Intel with images, photos, and stories of the people who would never make it to the corridors of the corporation. We have tried to give them voice. For all of you, I hope that this might mean owning being experts and managing the power it accords you — but with humility not arrogance. I hope it means asking the hard questions and not giving the easy answers. And I hope it means telling complicated stories, not just delivering sound bites. But most of all, I hope it means speaking truth to power.

And we have a lot of that to do.

For many of you, the next part of your life will unfold here, in the United States, and here we are in a moment of extraordinary flux. It might even be historic. Our daily papers (and news Web sites) carry stories about new market dynamics and dependencies, an economic recession, a renewed interest in sustainability and resource management, shifting global forces and relationships, and the prospect of a change, any change, in the White House. Running through all these stories, sometimes warp, sometimes weft, are new technologies. The Internet, mobile phones, social networking, virtual worlds, email, digital images, gaming consoles, and even spam, zombies, and viruses are all implicated.

For those of us who work at the intersections of everyday life and technology development, we have a responsibility to make these stories more complicated. We should tell the stories about the role the Internet plays in shaping our world, but we must also tell the stories about how the Internet isn't really changing anything. We have to be critical and smart and engaged. We have to create and nurture the places to ask questions and the people who can do so.

Now I know those are big asks. And I remember what it feels like to be at commencement and just to be grateful I survived the process. But one of things about rites of passage is that accompanying all that celebration is also the bestowing of new roles and responsibilities. I hope you find them as challenging and as liberating as I did. And I hope my little bit of anthropological advice helps. For this is how I want to know the world: present, vulnerable, curious, and brave. And it is how, if I could have my way, that you would all know it, too!

What the Future Will Bring

Ray Kurzweil

Ray Kurzweil is one of the leading pioneers in the field of AI (artificial intelligence). He was the principal developer of the first omni-font optical character recognition (OCR), the first print-to-speech reading machine for the blind, the first CCD flat-bed scanner, the first text-to-speech synthesizer, the first music synthesizer capable of recreating the grand piano and other orchestral instruments, and the first commercially marketed large-vocabulary speech recognition. Mr. Kurzweil has successfully founded and developed nine businesses in OCR, music synthesis, speech recognition, reading technology, virtual reality, financial investment, cybernetic art, and other areas of artificial intelligence. He was inducted in 2002 into the National Inventors Hall of Fame. In addition to receiving the 2015 Technical Grammy Award for outstanding achievements in the field of music technology, Mr. Kurzweil is the recipient of the National Medal of Technology, and holds twenty honorary Doctorates. He is a Director of Engineering at Google, heading up a team developing machine intelligence and natural language understanding.

What the Future Will Bring

Ray Kurzweil

In his 2005 commencement address at Worcester Polytechnic Institute, Ray Kurzweil offers a look at the "three great revolutions" that will have a major impact on our lives.

I've actually spent a few decades thinking about the future, trying to model technology trends. I'd like to share my ideas with you on what the future will hold, which will be rather different and empowering in terms of our ability to create knowledge, more so than many people realize.

I started thinking about the future and trying to anticipate it because of my interest in being an inventor myself. I realized that my inventions had to make sense when I finished a project, which would be three or four years later, and the world would be a different place. Everything would be different — the channels of distribution, the development tools. Most inventions, most technology projects fail not because the R&D department can't get it to work — if you read business plans, 90 percent of those groups will do exactly what they say if they're given the opportunity, yet 90 percent of those projects will still fail because the timing is wrong. Not all the enabling factors will be in place when they're needed. So realizing that, I began to try to model technology trends, attempting to anticipate where technology will be. This has taken on a life of its own. I have a team of ten people that gathers data in many different fields and we try to build mathematical models of what the future will look like.

Now, people say you can't predict the future. And for some things that turns out to be true. If you ask me, "Will the stock price of Google be higher or lower three years from now?" that's hard to predict. What will the next wireless common standard be? WiMAX, G-3, CDMA? That's hard to predict. But if you ask me, "What will the cost of a MIPS of computing be in 2010?" or "How much will it cost to sequence a base pair of DNA in 2012?" or "What will the special and temporal resolution of non-invasive brain scanning be in 2014?," I can give you a figure and it's likely to be accurate because we've been making these predictions for several decades based on these models. There's smooth, exponential growth in the power of these information technologies and computation that goes back a century — very smooth, exponential growth, basically doubling the power of electronics and communication every year. That's a 50 percent deflation rate.

The same thing is true in biology. It took us fifteen years to sequence HIV. We sequenced SARS in thirty-one days. We'll soon be able to sequence a virus in just a few days' time. We're basically doubling the power of these technologies every year.

And that's going to lead to three great revolutions that sometimes go by the letters GNR: genetics, nanotechnology, and robotics. Let me describe these briefly and talk about the implications for our lives ahead.

G, genetics, which is really a term for biotechnology, means that we are gaining the tools to actually understand biology as information processes and reprogram them. Now, 99 percent of the drugs that are on the market today were not done that way. They were done through drug discovery, basically finding something. "Oh, here's something that lowers blood pressure." We have no idea why it works or how it works and invariably it has lots of side effects, similar to primitive man and woman when they discovered their first tools. "Oh, here's a rock, this will make a good hammer."

But we didn't have the means of shaping the tools to actually do a job. We're now understanding the information processes underlying disease and aging and getting the tools to reprogram them.

We have little software programs inside us called genes, about 23,000 of them. They were designed or evolved tens of thousands of years ago when conditions were quite different. I'll give you just one example. The fat insulin receptor gene says, "Hold on to every calorie because the next hunting season may not work out so well." And that's a gene we'd like to reprogram. It made sense 20,000 years ago when calories were few and far between. What would happen if we blocked that? We have a new technology that can turn genes off called RNA interference. So when that gene was turned off in mice, these mice ate ravenously and yet they remained slim. They got the health benefits of being slim. They didn't get diabetes, didn't get heart disease or cancer. They lived 20 to 25 percent longer while eating ravenously. There are several pharmaceutical companies who have noticed that might be a good human drug.

There are many other genes we'd like to turn off. There are genes that are necessary for atherosclerosis, the cause of heart disease, to progress. There are genes that cancer relies on to progress. If we can turn these genes off, we could turn these diseases off. Turning genes off is just one of the methodologies. There are new forms of gene therapy that actually add genes so we'll not just have designer babies but designer baby boomers. And you probably read the Korean announcement of a new form of cell therapy where we can actually create new cells with your DNA so if you need a new heart or new heart cells you will be able to grow them with your own DNA, have them DNA-corrected, and thereby rejuvenate all your cells and tissues.

Ten or fifteen years from now, which is not that far away, these biotechnology techniques will have matured and we'll dramatically overcome the major diseases that we've struggled with for eons. These techniques will also allow us to slow down, stop, and even reverse aging processes.

The next revolution is nanotechnology, where we're applying information technology to matter and energy. We'll be able to overcome major problems that human civilization has struggled with. For example, energy. We have a little bit of sunlight here today. If we captured .03 percent, that's three ten-thousandths of the sunlight that falls on the Earth, we could meet all of our energy needs. We can't do that today because solar panels are very heavy, expensive, and inefficient. New nano-engineered designs, designed at the molecular level, will enable us to create very inexpensive, very efficient, lightweight solar panels, and to store the energy in nano-engineered fuel cells, which are highly decentralized, and meet all of our energy needs.

The killer app of nanotechnology is something called nano-bots, basically little robots the size of blood cells. If that sounds very futuristic, there are four major conferences on that already and they're already performing therapeutic functions in animals. One scientist cured Type-1 diabetes with these blood cell-sized nano-engineered capsules.

In regard to the 2020s, these devices will be able to go inside the human body and keep us healthy by destroying pathogens, correcting DNA errors, killing cancer cells, and so on, and even go into the brain and interact with our biological neurons. If that sounds futuristic, there are already neural implants that are FDA-approved, so there are people walking around who have computers in their brains and the biological neurons in their vicinity are perfectly happy to interact with these computerized devices. And the latest generation of the neural implant for Parkinson's disease allows the patients to download new software to their neural implant from outside themselves. By the 2020s, we'll be able to greatly enhance human intelligence, provide full-immersion virtual reality, for example, from within the nervous system using these types of technologies.

And finally R, which stands for robotics, which is really artificial intelligence at the human level; we'll see that in the late 2020s. By that time this exponential growth of computation will provide computer systems that are more powerful than the human brain. We'll have completed the reverse engineering of the human brain to get the software algorithms, the secrets, the principles of operation of how human intelligence works. A side benefit of that is we'll have greater insight into ourselves, how human intelligence works, how our emotional intelligence works, what human dysfunction is all about. We'll be able to correct, for example, neurological diseases and also expand human intelligence. And this is not going to be an alien invasion of intelligent machines. We already routinely do things in our civilization that would be impossible without our computer intelligence. If all the AI programs, narrow AI, embedded in our economic infrastructure were to stop today, our human civilization would grind to a halt. So we're already very integrated with our technology. Computer technology used to be very remote. Now we carry it in our pockets. It'll soon be in our clothing. It's already begun migrating into our bodies and brains. We will become increasingly intimate with our technology.

The implications of all this is we will extend human longevity. We've already done that. A thousand years ago, human life expectancy was about twenty-three. So most of you would be senior citizens if this were taking place a thousand years ago. In 1800, two hundred years ago, human life expectancy was thirty-seven. So most of you parents, including myself, wouldn't be here. It was fifty years in 1900. It's now pushing eighty. Every time there's been some advance in technology we've pushed it forward: sanitation, antibiotics. This biotechnology revolution will expand it again. Nanotechnology will solve problems that we don't get around to with biotechnology. We'll have dramatic expansion of human longevity.

But actually life would get boring if we were sitting around for a few hundred years — we would be doing the same things over and over again — unless we had radical life expansion. And this technology will also expand our opportunities, expand our ability to create and appreciate knowledge. And creating knowledge is what the human species is all about. We're the only species that has knowledge that we pass down from generation to generation. That's what we will continue doing indefinitely. We are expanding exponentially human knowledge and that is really what is exciting about the future.

I've tried to share my vision with you, and some practical advice. And my practical advice is that creating knowledge is what will be most exciting in life. And in order to create knowledge you have to have passion. So find a challenge that you can be passionate about, and there are many of them that are worthwhile. And if you're passionate about a worthwhile challenge, you can find the ideas to overcome that challenge. Those ideas exist and you can find them. And persistence usually pays off. You've all had timed tests where you had two or three hours to complete a test. But the tests in life are not timed. If you need an extra hour you can take it. Or an extra day, an extra week, an extra year, an extra decade. You're the only one that will determine your own success or failure. Thomas Edison tried thousands of filaments to get his light bulb to work and none of them worked. And he easily could have said, "I guess all those skeptics who said that a practical light bulb was impossible were right." Obviously he didn't do that. You know the rest of the story.

If you have a challenge that you feel passionately about that's really worthwhile, then you should never give in. To quote Winston Churchill, "Never give in. Never give in. Never, never, never, never, in nothing great or small, large or petty, never give in."

I wish all of you long lives — very long lives — of success, creativity, health, and happiness. And may the Force be with you.

The Impoverishment of American Culture

Dana Gioia

DANA GIOIA is a poet and critic. Born in Los Angles of Italian and Mexican ancestry, he attended Stanford and Harvard before taking a detour into business. After years of writing and reading late in the evenings after work, he quit a corporate vice presidency in 1992 to write. He has published four collections of poetry, *Daily Horoscope* (1986), *The Gods of Winter* (1991), *Interrogations at Noon* (2001), which won the American Book Award, and *Pity the Beautiful* (2012); and three critical volumes, including the influential study *Can Poetry Matter?* (1992). Mr. Gioia has taught at Johns Hopkins, Sarah Lawrence, Wesleyan (Connecticut), Mercer, and Colorado College. From 2003-2009 he served as the Chairman of the National Endowment for the Arts. At the NEA he created the largest literary programs in federal history, including Shakespeare in American Communities and Poetry Out Loud, as well as The Big Read, which helped reverse a quarter century of decline in U.S. reading. He was awarded the Laetare Medal in 2010. He is currently the Judge Widney Professor of Poetry and Public Culture at the University of Southern California.

The Impoverishment of American Culture

Dana Gioia

In his 2007 commencement address at Stanford University, Dana Gioia proposes ways to reverse our country's "colossal cultural and political decline."

A person never really escapes his or her childhood. At heart I'm still a working-class kid — half Italian, half Mexican — from L.A., or more precisely from Hawthorne, a city that you may know only as the setting of Quentin Tarantino's *Pulp Fiction* and *Jackie Brown* — two films that capture the ineffable charm of my hometown.

I hope you will indulge me for beginning on a personal note. I am the first person in my family ever to attend college, and I owe my education to my father, who sacrificed nearly everything to give his four children the best education possible. My dad had a fairly hard life. He never spoke English until he went to school. He barely survived a plane crash in World War II. He worked hard, but never had much success, except with his family.

When I was about twelve, my dad told me that he hoped I would go to Stanford, a place I had never heard of. For him, Stanford represented every success he had missed yet wanted for his children. He would be proud of me today — no matter how dull my speech.

I loved my mother dearly, but she could be a challenge. For example, when she learned I had been nominated to be chairman of the National Endowment for the Arts, she phoned and said, "Don't think I'm impressed."

I know that there was a bit of controversy when my name was announced as the graduation speaker. A few students were especially concerned that I lacked celebrity status. It seemed I wasn't famous enough. I couldn't agree more. As I have often told my wife and children, "I'm simply not famous enough."

And that — in a more general and less personal sense — is the subject I want to address today, the fact that we live in a culture that barely acknowledges and rarely celebrates the arts or artists.

There is an experiment I'd love to conduct. I'd like to survey a cross-section of Americans and ask them how many active NBA players, Major League Baseball players, and *American Idol* finalists they can name.

Then I'd ask them how many living American poets, playwrights, painters, sculptors, architects, classical musicians, conductors, and composers they can name.

I'd even like to ask how many living American scientists or social thinkers they can name.

Fifty years ago, I suspect that along with Mickey Mantle, Willie Mays, and Sandy Koufax, most Americans could have named, at the very least, Robert Frost, Carl Sandburg, Arthur Miller, Thornton Wilder, Georgia O'Keeffe, Leonard Bernstein, Leontyne Price, and Frank Lloyd Wright. Not to mention scientists and thinkers like Linus Pauling, Jonas Salk, Rachel Carson, Margaret Mead, and especially Dr. Alfred Kinsey.

I don't think that Americans were smarter then, but American culture was. Even the mass media placed a greater emphasis on presenting a broad range of human achievement.

I grew up mostly among immigrants, many of whom never learned to speak English. But at night watching TV variety programs like *The Ed Sullivan Show* or *The Perry Como Music Hall*, I saw — along with comedians, popular singers, and movie stars — classical musicians like Jascha Heifetz and Arthur Rubinstein, opera singers like Robert Merrill and Anna Moffo, and jazz greats like Duke Ellington and Louis Armstrong captivate an audience of millions with their art.

The same was even true of literature. I first encountered Robert Frost, John Steinbeck, Lillian Hellman, and James Baldwin on general interest TV shows. All of these people were famous to the average American — because the culture considered them important.

Today no working-class or immigrant kid would encounter that range of arts and ideas in the popular culture. Almost everything in our national culture, even the news, has been reduced to entertainment, or altogether eliminated.

The loss of recognition for artists, thinkers, and scientists has impoverished our culture in innumerable ways, but let me mention one. When virtually all of a culture's celebrated figures are in sports or entertainment, how few possible role models we offer the young.

There are so many other ways to lead a successful and meaningful life that are not denominated by money or fame. Adult life begins in a child's imagination, and we've relinquished that imagination to the marketplace.

Of course, I'm not forgetting that politicians can also be famous, but it is interesting how our political process grows more like the entertainment industry each year. When a successful guest appearance on *The Colbert Report* becomes more important than passing legislation, democracy gets scary.

No wonder Hollywood considers politics "show business for ugly people."

Everything now is entertainment. And the purpose of this omnipresent commercial entertainment is to sell us something. American culture has mostly become one vast infomercial.

I have a reccurring nightmare. I am in Rome visiting the Sistine Chapel. I look up at Michelangelo's incomparable fresco of *The Creation of Man.* I see God stretching out his arm to touch the reclining Adam's finger. And then I notice in the other hand Adam is holding a Diet Pepsi.

When was the last time you have seen a featured guest on David Letterman or Jay Leno who isn't trying to sell you something? A new movie, a new TV show, a new book, or a new vote?

Don't get me wrong. I love entertainment, and I love the free market. I have a Stanford MBA and spent fifteen years in the food industry. I adore my big-screen TV. The productivity and efficiency of the free market are beyond dispute. It has created a society of unprecedented prosperity.

But we must remember that the marketplace does only one thing — it puts a price on everything.

The role of culture, however, must go beyond economics. It is not focused on the price of things, but on their value. And, above all, culture should tell us what is beyond price, including what does not belong in the marketplace. A culture should also provide some cogent view of the good life beyond mass accumulation. In this respect, our culture is failing us.

There is only one social force in America potentially large and strong enough to counterbalance this profit-driven commercialization of cultural values, our educational system, especially public education. Traditionally, education has been one thing that our nation has agreed cannot be left entirely to the marketplace — but made mandatory and freely available to everyone.

At fifty-six, I am just old enough to remember a time when every public high school in this country had a music program with choir and band, usually a jazz band, too, sometimes even orchestra. And every high school offered a drama program, sometimes with dance instruction. And there were writing opportunities in the school paper and literary magazine, as well as studio art training.

I am sorry to say that these programs are no longer widely available to the new generation of Americans. This once visionary and democratic system has been almost entirely dismantled by well-meaning but myopic school boards, county commissioners, and state officials, with the federal government largely indifferent to the issue. Art became an expendable luxury, and fifty million students have paid the price. Today, a child's access to arts education is largely a function of his or her parents' income.

In a time of social progress and economic prosperity, why have we experienced this colossal cultural and political decline? There are several reasons, but I must risk offending many friends and colleagues by saying that surely artists and intellectuals are partly to blame. Most American artists, intellectuals, and academics have lost their ability to converse with the rest of society. We have become wonderfully expert in talking to one another, but we have become almost invisible and inaudible in the general culture.

This mutual estrangement has had enormous cultural, social, and political consequences. America needs its artists and intellectuals, and they need to reestablish their rightful place in the general culture. If we could reopen the conversation between our best minds and the broader public, the results would not only transform society but also artistic and intellectual life.

There is no better place to start this rapprochement than in arts education. How do we explain to the larger society the benefits of this civic investment when they have been convinced that the purpose of arts education is mostly to produce more artists — hardly a compelling argument to either the average taxpayer or financially strapped school board?

We need to create a new national consensus. The purpose of arts education is not to produce more artists, though that is a by-product. The real purpose of arts education is to create complete human beings capable of leading successful and productive lives in a free society.

This is not happening now in American schools. Even if you forget the larger catastrophe that only 70 percent of American kids now graduate from high school, what are we to make of a public education system whose highest goal seems to be producing minimally competent entry-level workers?

The situation is a cultural and educational disaster, but it also has huge and alarming economic consequences. If the United States is to compete effectively with the rest of the world in the new global marketplace, it is not going to succeed through cheap labor or cheap raw materials, nor even the free flow of capital or a streamlined industrial base. To compete successfully, this country needs continued creativity, ingenuity, and innovation.

It is hard to see those qualities thriving in a nation whose educational system ranks at the bottom of the developed world and has mostly eliminated the arts from the curriculum.

I have seen firsthand the enormous transformative power of the arts — in the lives of individuals, in communities, and even society at large.

Marcus Aurelius believed that the course of wisdom consisted of learning to trade easy pleasures for more complex and challenging ones. I worry about a culture that, bit by bit, trades off the challenging pleasures of art for the easy comforts of entertainment. And that is exactly what is happening — not just in the media, but in our schools and civic life.

Entertainment promises us a predictable pleasure — humor, thrills, emotional titillation, or even the odd delight of being vicariously terrified. It exploits and manipulates who we are rather than challenges us with a vision of who we might become. A child who spends a month mastering *Halo* or *NBA Live* on Xbox has not been awakened and transformed the way that child would be spending the time rehearsing a play or learning to draw.

If you don't believe me, you should read the statistical studies that are now coming out about American civic participation. Our country is dividing into two distinct behavioral groups.

One group spends most of its free time sitting at home as passive consumers of electronic entertainment. Even family communication is breaking down as members increasingly spend their time alone, staring at their individual screens.

The other group also uses and enjoys the new technology, but these individuals balance it with a broader range of activities. They go out — to exercise, play sports, volunteer and do charity work at about three times the level of the first group. By every measure they are vastly more active and socially engaged than the first group.

What is the defining difference between passive and active citizens? Curiously, it isn't income, geography, or even education. It depends on whether or not they read for pleasure and participate in the arts. These cultural activities seem to awaken a heightened sense of individual awareness and social responsibility.

Why do these issues matter to you? This is the culture you are about to enter. Those of you who've had the privilege of attending college have been part of a community that takes arts and ideas seriously. Even if you spent most of your free time watching *Grey's Anatomy*, playing *Guitar Hero*, or Facebooking your friends, those important endeavors were balanced by courses and conversations about literature, politics, technology, and ideas.

You now face the choice of whether you want to be a passive consumer or an active citizen. Do you want to watch the world on a screen or live in it so meaningfully that you change it?

That's no easy task, so don't forget what the arts provide.

Art is an irreplaceable way of understanding and expressing the world — equal to but distinct from scientific and conceptual methods. Art addresses us in the fullness of our being — simultaneously speaking to our intellect, emotions, intuition, imagination, memory, and physical senses. There are some truths about life that can be expressed only as stories, or songs, or images.

Art delights, instructs, consoles. It educates our emotions. And it remembers. As Robert Frost once said about poetry, "It is a way of remembering that which it would impoverish us to forget." Art awakens, enlarges, refines, and restores our humanity. You don't outgrow art. The same work can mean something different at each stage of your life. A good book changes as you change.

My own art is poetry, though my current daily life sometimes makes me forget that. So let me end my remarks with a short poem.

PRAISE TO THE RITUALS THAT CELEBRATE CHANGE

Praise to the rituals that celebrate change,
old robes worn for new beginnings,
solemn protocol where the mutable soul,
surrounded by ancient experience, grows
young in the imagination's white dress.

Because it is not the rituals we honor
but our trust in what they signify, these rites
that honor us as witnesses — whether to watch
lovers swear loyalty in a careless world
or a newborn washed with water and oil.

So praise to innocence — impulsive and evergreen —
and let the old be touched by youth's
wayward astonishment at learning something new,
and dream of a future so fitting and so just
that our desire will bring it into being.

Commencement Address

Muhammad Yunus

PROFESSOR MUHAMMAD YUNUS is the distinguished recipient of the 2006 Nobel Peace Prize. He is the founder and managing director of Grameen Bank of Dhaka, Bangladesh. Dr. Yunus is internationally recognized for developing microfinancing for low-income families as a way to break the vicious cycle of poverty, and to help productive enterprises to grow and communities to prosper. Nelson Mandela praised him as "someone who feels deeply about working for peace and justice around the world."

Commencement Address

Muhammad Yunus

In his 2008 commencement address at MIT, Dr. Muhammad Yunus advocates "changing the course of the world" through the creation of socially conscious businesses.

What a wonderful feeling to be here today. To be with all of you, some of the brightest minds in the world, right at a moment when you decide the path you will embark on in life. You represent the future of the world. The choices that you will make for yourself will decide the fate of mankind. This is how it has always been. Sometimes we are aware of it, most of the time we are not. I hope you'll remain aware of it and make an effort to be remembered not simply as a creative generation but as a socially conscious creative generation. Try it.

I had no idea whether my life would someday be relevant to anyone else's. But in the mid-seventies, out of frustration with the terrible economic situation in Bangladesh, I decided to see if I could make myself useful to one poor person a day in the village next door to the university campus where I was teaching. I found myself in an unfamiliar situation. Out of necessity I had to find a way out. Since I did not have a road-map, I had to fall back on my basic instinct to do that. At any moment I could have withdrawn myself from my unknown path, but I did not. I stubbornly went on to find my own way. Luckily, at the end, I found it. That was microcredit and Grameen Bank.

Now, in hindsight, I can joke about it. When people ask me, "How did you figure out all the rules and procedures that is now known as Grameen system?" my answer is: "That was very simple and easy. Whenever I needed a rule or a procedure in our work, I just looked at the conventional banks to see what they do in a similar situation. Once I learned what they did, I just did the opposite." That's how I got our rules. Conventional banks go to the rich, we go to the poor; their rule is — "the more you have, the more you get." So our rule became — "the less you have, the higher attention you get. If you have nothing, you get the highest priority." They ask for collateral, we abandoned it, as if we had never heard of it. They need lawyers in their business, we don't. No lawyer is involved in any of our loan transactions. They are owned by the rich, ours is owned by the poorest, the poorest women to boot. I can go on adding more to this list to show how Grameen does things quite the opposite way.

Was it really a systematic policy — to do it the opposite way? No, it wasn't. But that's how it turned out ultimately, because our objective was different. I had not even noticed it until a senior banker admonished me by saying: "Dr. Yunus, you are trying to put the banking system upside down." I quickly agreed with him. I said: "Yes, because the banking system is standing on its head."

I could not miss seeing the ruthlessness of moneylenders in the village. First I lent the money to replace the loan-sharks. Then I went to the local bank to request them to lend money to the poor. They refused.

After months of deadlock I persuaded them by offering myself as a guarantor. This is how microcredit was born in 1976. Today Grameen Bank lends money to 7.5 million borrowers, 97 percent women. They own the bank. The bank has lent out over $7.0 billion in Bangladesh over the years. Globally 130 million poor families receive microcredit. Even then banks have not changed much. They do not mind writing off a trillion dollars in a sub-prime crisis, but they still stay away from lending $100 (U.S. dollars) to a poor woman despite the fact such loans have near 100 percent repayment record globally.

While focusing on microcredit we saw the need for other types of interventions to help the rural population, in general, and the poor, in particular. We tried our interventions in the health sector, information technology, renewable energy, and on several other fronts.

Since we worked with poor women, health issues quickly drew our attention. We introduced health insurance. We succeeded in developing an effective healthcare program based on health insurance, but have not been able to expand this program because of non-availability of doctors. Doctors are reluctant to stay in the villages. (It has become such a big bottleneck that we have now decided to set up a medical college to produce doctors.) Under the program a villager pays about $2.00 (U.S. dollars) a year as a health insurance premium, to get health coverage for the entire family. Financially, it is sustainable.

I became a strong believer in the power of information technology to change the lives of poor people. This encouraged me to create a cell phone company called Grameen Phone. We brought phones to the villages of Bangladesh and gave loans to the poor women to buy themselves cell phones to sell their service and make money. It became an instant success.

Seventy percent of the population of Bangladesh do not have access to electricity. We wanted to address this issue by introducing solar home systems in the villages. We created a separate company called Grameen Shakti, or Grameen

Energy. It became a very successful company in popularizing solar home systems, bio-gas, and environment-friendly cooking stoves. It has already reached 155,000 homes with solar home systems, and aims to reach one million homes by 2012. As we started creating a series of companies around renewable energy, information technology, textile, agriculture, livestock, education, health, finance, etc., I was wondering why conventional businesses do not see business the way we see it. They have different goals than ours. We design our businesses one way, they design theirs in another way.

Conventional businesses are based on the theoretical framework provided by the designers of capitalist economic system. In this framework 'business' has to be a profit-maximizing entity. The more aggressively a business pursues it, the better the system functions — we are told. The bigger the profit, the more successful the business is; the more happy investors are. In my work it never occurred to me that I should maximize profit. All my struggle was to take each of my enterprises to a level where it could at least be self-sustaining. I defined the mission of my businesses in a different way than that of the traditional businesses.

As I was doing it, obviously I was violating the basic tenet of capitalist system — profit maximization. Since I was engaged in finding my own solution to reach the mission of my business, I was not looking at any existing road maps. My only concern was to see if my path was taking me where I wanted to go. When it worked I felt very happy. I know maximization of profit makes people happy. I don't maximize profit, but my businesses are a great source of my happiness. If you had done what I have done you would be very happy too! I am convinced that profit maximization is not the only source of happiness in business. "Business" has been interpreted too narrowly in the existing framework of capitalism. This interpretation is based on the assumption that a human being is a single dimensional being. His business-related happiness is related to the size of the profit he makes. He is presented as a robot-like money-making machine.

But we all know that real-life human beings are multidimensional beings — not unidimensional like the theory assumes. For a real-life human being money-making is a means, not an end. But for the businessman in the existing theory, money-making is both a means and also an end.

This narrow interpretation has done us great damage. All business people around the world have been imitating this one-dimensional theoretical businessman as precisely as they can to make sure they get the most from the capitalist system. If you are a businessman you have to wear profit-maximizing glasses all the time. As a result, the only thing you see in the world are the profit-enhancing opportunities. Important problems that we face in the world cannot be addressed because profit-maximizing eyes cannot see them.

We can easily reformulate the concept of a businessman to bring him closer to a real human being. In order to take into account the multidimensionality of real human beings, we may assume that there are two distinct sources of happiness in the business world — 1) maximizing profit, and 2) achieving some pre-defined social objective. Since there are clear conflicts between the two objectives, the business world will have to be made up of two different kinds of businesses — 1) profit-maximizing business, and 2) social business. The specific type of happiness will come from the specific type of business.

Then an investor will have two choices — he can invest in one or in both. My guess is most people will invest in both in various proportions. This means people will use two sets of eyeglasses — profit-maximizing glasses, and social-business glasses. This will bring a big change in the world. Profit-maximizing businessmen will be amazed to see how different the world looks once they take off the profit-maximizing glasses and wear the social-business glasses. By looking at the world from two different perspectives, business decision-makers will be able to decide better, act better, and these decisions and actions will lead to a dramatically better world.

While I was wondering whether the idea of social business would make any sense to the corporate world, I had an opportunity to talk to the chairman of Danone Group, Mr. Franck Riboud, about this subject. It made perfect sense to him right away. Together we created Grameen Danone company as a social business in Bangladesh. This company produces yogurt fortified with micro-nutrients which are missing in the malnourished children of Bangladesh. Because it is a social business, Grameen and Danone will never take any dividend out of the company beyond recouping the initial investment. The bottom line for the company is to see how many children overcome their nutrition deficiency each year.

The next initiative came from Crédit Agricole of France. We created Grameen Crédit Agricole Microfinance Foundation to provide financial support to microfinance organizations and social businesses.

We created a small water company to provide good quality drinking water in a cluster of villages of Bangladesh. This is a joint venture with Veolia, a leading water company in the world. Bangladesh has a terrible drinking-water problem. In a large part of Bangladesh tubewell water is highly arsenic-contaminated, surface water is polluted. This social-business water company will be a prototype for supplying safe drinking water in a sustainable and affordable way to people who are faced with water crisis. Once it is perfected, it can be replicated in other villages, within Bangladesh and outside.

We have already established an eye-care hospital specializing in cataract operations, with a capacity to undertake 10,000 operations per year. This is a joint-venture social business with the Green Children Foundation created by two singers in their early twenties, Tom and Milla, from England and Norway.

We have signed a joint-venture agreement with Intel Corporation, to create a social-business company called Grameen-Intel to bring information technology–based services to the poor in healthcare, marketing, education, and remittances.

We also signed a social-business joint-venture agreement with Saudi German Hospital Group to set up a series of hospitals in Bangladesh.

Many more companies from around the world are showing interest in such social-business joint ventures. A leading shoe company wants to create a social business to make sure that nobody goes without shoes. One leading pharmaceutical company wishes to set up a joint-venture social-business company to produce nutritional supplements appropriate for Bangladeshi pregnant mothers and young women, at the cheapest possible price.

We are also in discussion to launch a social-business company to produce chemically treated mosquito-nets to protect people in Bangladesh and Africa from malaria and other mosquito-borne diseases.

Your generation can bring a breakthrough in changing the course of the world. You can be the socially conscious creative generation that the world is waiting for. You can bring your creativity to design brilliant social businesses to overcome poverty, disease, environmental degradation, food crisis, depletion of non-renewable resources, etc. Each one of you is capable of changing the world. To make a start all that each one of you has to do is to design a business plan for a social business. Each prototype of a social business can be a cute little business. But if it works out, the whole world can be changed by replicating it in thousands of locations.

Prototype development is the key. In designing a prototype all we need is a socially oriented creative mind. That could be each one of you. No matter what you do in your life, make it a point to design or be involved with at least one social business to address one problem that depresses you the most. If you have the design and the money, go ahead and put it into action. I can tell you very emphatically that in terms of human capability there is no difference between a poor person and a very privileged person. All human beings are packed with unlimited potential. Poor people are no exception to this rule. But the world around them never gave them the opportunity to know that each of them is carrying a wonderful gift in them. The gift remains unknown and unwrapped. Our challenge is to help the poor unwrap their gift.

Poverty is not created by the poor. It is created by the system. Poverty is an artificial imposition on people. Once you fall outside the system, it works against you. It makes it very difficult to return to the system.

How do we change this? Where do we begin?

Three basic interventions will make a big difference in the existing system: a) broadening the concept of business by including "social business" into the framework of marketplace; b) creating inclusive financial and healthcare services, which can reach out to every person on the planet; c) designing appropriate information technology devices and services for the bottom-most people and making them easily available to them.

Your generation has the opportunity to make a break with the past and create a beautiful new world. We see the ever-growing problems created by the individual-centered aggressively accumulative economy. If we let it proceed without serious modifications, we may soon reach the point of no return. Among other things, this type of economy has placed our planet under serious threat through climatic distortions. Single-minded pursuit of profit has made us forget that this planet is our home; that we are supposed to make it safe and beautiful, not make it more unlivable everyday by promoting a lifestyle, which ignores all warnings of safety.

At this point let me give you the good news. No matter how daunting the problems look, don't get browbeaten by their size. Big problems are most often just an aggregation of tiny problems. Get to the smallest component of the problem. Then it becomes an innocent bite-size problem, and you can have all the fun dealing with it. You'll be thrilled to see in how many ways you can crack it. You can tame it or make it disappear by various social and economic actions, including social business. Pick out the action that looks most efficient in the given circumstances. Tackling big problems does not always have to be through giant actions or global initiatives or big businesses. It can start as a tiny little action. If you shape it the right way, it can grow into a global action in no time. Even the biggest problem can be cracked by a small, well-designed intervention. That's where you and your creativity come in. These interventions can be so small that each one of you can crack these problems right from your garage. If you have a friend or two to work with you, it is all the better. It can be fun too.

You are born in the age of ideas. Ideas are something I am sure your generation will not run out of. The question I am raising now is — what use will you want to make of them? Make money by selling or using your ideas? Or change the world with your ideas? Or do both? It is up to you to decide.

There are two clear tasks in front of you — 1) to end poverty in the world once for all, and 2) to set the world in the right path to undo all the damage we have done to the environment by our ignorance and selfishness. The time is right. Your initiatives can produce big results, even lead you to achieving these goals. Then yours will be the most successful generation in human history. You will take your grandchildren to the poverty museums with tremendous pride that your generation had finally made it happen.

Congratulations on being part of a generation that has exciting possibilities, and advance congratulations to you all for your future successes in creating a new world where everyone on this planet can stand tall as a human being.

The Virtue of Varied Perspectives

Kathryn D. Sullivan

KATHRYN D. SULLIVAN, PH.D., is a distinguished scientist, renowned astronaut, and intrepid explorer. Dr. Sullivan was confirmed by the U. S. Senate as the Under Secretary of Commerce for Oceans and Atmosphere and NOAA Administrator on March 6, 2014, having served as Acting NOAA Administrator since February 28, 2013. Dr. Sullivan was one of the first six women selected to join the NASA astronaut corps in 1978 and holds the distinction of being the first American woman to walk in space.

The Virtue of Varied Perspectives

Kathryn D. Sullivan

In her 2015 commencement address at American University College of Arts and Sciences, Kathryn D. Sullivan offers her insights about how "the experience of being in space led me to understand that the most pressing challenges of my world were in fact those that face us all collectively."

Graduations always remind me of the first time I sat on the launch pad at the Kennedy Space Center aboard the Space Shuttle Challenger. You didn't expect that analogy, did you?

Like all of you, I was dressed up that day in an uncomfortable, foreign outfit, forced to listen to a bunch of people as they droned their way through an elaborate ritual that just would not end. And like you, the anticipation of what was about to happen to me was a bit overwhelming; preparing to be thrust into uncharted territories, exhilarated yet mildly terrified for what was to come. Like a lot of you, I suspect, I questioned if I was really ready for what lay ahead.

Sure, I knew every detail of the countdown procedure that was unfolding around us, and of course I was well-versed in all the scientific experiments I was responsible for, not to mention how thoroughly I understood every detail of the spacesuit that would protect me when I floated outside the shuttle.

But I still couldn't help but wonder if all my hard work and extensive technical training had truly prepared me for my next step as the first American woman to walk in space.

Okay, before I, too, start droning on, let's turn it back to you for a bit, shall we? American University has provided all of you with opportunities that have fostered your intellectual development, your creativity, and your spirit. And today, you are united by that common experience.

But the real strength you take with you today comes from the diversity of perspectives amongst you. As I look out upon this assembly, I see future leaders, eager to develop solutions to the problems of today and take on the challenges of tomorrow. For each of you, today is undoubtedly a day filled with joy, relief, and a tremendous amount of satisfaction. It's the culmination of a four, or in a few cases, five-year journey. But for one of you, this journey took a lot longer. About thirty-one years longer.

Since taking his first higher education class thirty-five years ago, Steve Gamble studied Buddhism in Nepal, got married, answered your innumerable questions at the University IT help desk, and never shied away from asking the hard questions. When asked what it means to walk across this stage, Steve didn't hesitate. He explained that his AU education instilled in him a more developed understanding of the world and a more vivid appreciation of life itself.

For a handful of parents, grandparents, aunts, and uncles in this audience, this is a very special day filled with great pride as you watch the very first member of your family receive a college degree. What a fabulous moment and tremendous achievement.

I suggest that today is not simply a day to celebrate what you have in common as the class of 2015, but also a day to revel in your differences, and to celebrate the environment that American University provided to foster learning about — and through — the exploration of those differences.

On this day, we celebrate more than just your journey to this moment. We celebrate the capacity this journey has instilled in you for the road ahead. A capacity, a hunger, to continue exploring new perspectives. And that's why I'm so excited to be speaking with you today.

At T-31 seconds, the elaborate countdown ritual at the Kennedy Space Center wrapped up and we got the final go for launch. Before we could blink, the shuttle leapt off the pad and we were off to infinity and beyond.

Any worries or hesitation I felt before, well, it was seriously too late now. Within minutes, we were over England, and I got my first glimpse of this little blue marble called Earth. I was overwhelmed by the beauty of our planet; entranced with how her interconnected systems ebb and flow with one another. From that vantage point one can hardly make out anything other than sea and land and atmosphere. Geographic borders are no more visible than are the individuals that live within them. That cosmic adventure introduced me to an entirely new perspective, one that dramatically shaped who I am today.

During your time at American University, you have been blessed with an environment that encouraged similar exploration, albeit with rather more gravity and certainly much better food.

AU has challenged you to engage with dissenting viewpoints, ones that prodded you to consider the world in a different way. And in doing so, this university shielded you from the danger of collective acceptance and complacency.

Today, this institution will hand each of you a diploma to recognize your achievement. You will be told that this document attests to your accomplishment and will prove to people — potential employers, for example — that you are ready and able to contribute to society. That's not quite right.

Your diploma is, after all, just a piece of paper. It does confirm that you completed a course of study with some degree of success. But that alone doesn't say anything about the value of what you gained at American University. There is one thing on your diploma that *does* speak to that, however. The only thing that speaks to that. And it is your name on that certificate.

Your name represents who you became in reaching for this recognition. It represents the sum of all the investments you made in growing towards this day. It embodies those late nights in Bender Library cramming for the next morning's exam. The thankless hours you spent working a dull job or interning on Capitol Hill. The resolve to press forward that you had to dig deep to muster after just barely passing a class in a subject far beyond your comfort zone. And the late nights you spent mastering a concept not because it was on a test, but because it had so completely captured your imagination and your interest. Also, your willingness to allow the differences you encountered to unite you with your colleagues and with other people rather than divide you. Your openness was present when you invited others to join you in the exploration of new points of view.

Your name on that diploma is also a reminder of the hard work and sacrifice invested on your behalf by the people who challenged and supported you during your journey to this moment. For, just like a rocket launch, college graduation is much more than a moment of individual achievement. In both instances, there are many people who helped us who are not in the spotlight. Many who stayed up late hours, struggled with the impossible, and put our quest before their own concerns.

Remember to thank those people today, and carry the lesson of their sacrifice with you on the next leg of life's journey. Pay their gift forward to others who are on grand or difficult journeys.

As of tomorrow, you will leave behind this wonderful space for intellectual exploration that has given you protection against complacency and group think. You are about to be ejected into a time of massive, turbulent, global transformation.

It's a time of strident and violent schisms along national, regional, and even tribal lines, and all of this is happening amid a systematic erosion of trust in public institutions. So, "next generation," how will you continue to grow through diversity?

To expand your horizons and refine your perspectives? To turn the knowledge you've gained into a force for good? Are you ready?

For me, the experience of being in space led me to understand that the most pressing challenges of my world were in fact those that face us all collectively. As I circled the world every ninety minutes for days on end, it became clear to me that all of us on Earth are inextricably linked to each other as humankind. There is no "I" or "them." We are one. And our very existence is completely dependent on the workings of that little blue marble that I could hold in the palm of my hand.

And so I came to believe that I owed it to myself and the people who put me in space to make good on that unique point of view. It was this newfound perspective that led me to leap into my next professional adventure: putting scientific understanding of the Earth to work for all of us.

When I returned to Earth, I built — not found — but *built* a career focused on achieving that outcome. My work at NOAA has allowed me to make good on the new frame of mind I developed in space; that the problems most pressing in our times and most vital for our future do not discriminate based on race, gender, or wealth. These great challenges, like so many of the past, can only be addressed by coming together and thinking of the generations yet to come. This will take listening to each other, learning, and reaching for new perspectives, precisely the habits of mind and learning that your experience at American University has instilled in you.

As a community, you have already proven your ability to check your personal agendas at the door and work towards productive solutions as a collective. You have been subjected to more diverse backgrounds, ideas, opinions, and experiences than many people will ever come to know. And I hope you have realized through this that it was only by taking the time to stop and listen that you were able to grow and learn. Your experience at AU has provided you with more than an academic credential. You head off into this world with ideas and ideals. With passion and purpose. With a strong sense of what it takes to build community and how vital community is to life.

I'm quite sure the answer to my earlier question about your readiness for the next step is *yes, you are well prepared for what lies ahead.* In due time you will surely forget Bernoulli's Principle, the construction of iambic pentameter, and the name of Monet's most famous Impressionist painting. But what you will not forget is what American University has instilled in you: the strong, burning hunger to broaden your lens.

We all must strive to never become complacent in our quest to seek out a more developed understanding of how our world works. And perspective is what allows us to find happiness and true meaning in our lives.

Your journey to new perspectives actually begins today.

I encourage you to search for controversy, for exploring contrasting points of view can be both revealing and catalytic. Use your ears more than your mouth, for learning can only happen when we pause to listen. Take the challenging path, always. And do not be afraid of change. Like gravity, it's just kind of everywhere; resistance is futile.

And always be a better neighbor. Not because it's expected of you, but because it makes you a better person, and you know it's the right thing to do.

The gift of education and the habit of exploration have prepared each of you to be leaders — in your careers, your communities, and your families. Cherish this, and make it count.

Communities that are made up of people who listen keenly, think deeply, and act wisely are perhaps the only ones that are able to create progress and peace.

We owe this to ourselves. We owe this to each other. And we owe this to the little blue marble called Earth.

Please know that each of you has my great admiration and full confidence as you take this next step. I congratulate you and wish you each the very best of luck.

With Apologies to the Gettysburg Address: May 20, 2007

Harold Prince

HAROLD PRINCE is a legendary, Tony Award–winning producer and director of some of the most important and popular Broadway musicals in the history of the American theater. As a producer, his hits include *Pajama Game*, *Damn Yankees*, *West Side Story*, and *Fiddler on the Roof*. He has produced and directed such innovative musicals as *Cabaret*, *Company*, *Follies*, *A Little Night Music*, and *Pacific Overtures,* and he has directed such favorites as *Sweeney Todd*, *Evita*, and *The Phantom of the Opera*. In 2006, he won a special Tony Award for Lifetime Achievement in the Theater.

With Apologies to the Gettysburg Address: May 20, 2007

Harold Prince

In his 2007 commencement address at Gettysburg College, Harold Prince champions "visible social activism," saying it "beats blogging every time."

Fourscore and seven years ago was 1920. I didn't arrive for another eight years. Where was the world in 1920?

Woodrow Wilson died, and was replaced by Warren Harding, who declared before his nomination, "America's present need is not heroics, but healing, not nostrums, but normalcy, not revolution, but restoration." Then he was elected president, and lost his message. In a big way. The 1920s generation was called The Lost Generation. Some were disgusted with nationalism, and others, the pacifists, lined up against the pro-military.

In 1920 the League of Nations met in Geneva, but without

the membership of the U.S., Russia, and the nations defeated in The Great War. In 1920, barely 20 percent of America's virgin forest land remained uncut. It was in 1920 that U.S. government agents, raiding thirty-three cities, rounded up thousands of persons suspected of subversive activity, many of whom were detained for long periods of time without ever being formally charged. And in 1920, a British mandate was established in Iraq. Muslim clerics in Baghdad began denouncing British rule, and for a time the Sunni and Shia tribes united in opposition of the west.

I've been around a long time — almost fourscore, but without the seven added. I had my first paying job sixty years ago. At that time, I met composers, lyricists, and playwrights with whom I would work for the body of my life. And the atmosphere in our society was so generous — and welcoming — that I also met and grew to know most of the great established writers, composers, and directors in the theater. They seemed curious about what I wanted to do with my life, and they asked questions and they listened to me. I have always believed that they were so forthcoming, not only because manners in those days were held in high regard, but because there were so many of them working consistently and simultaneously. The arts were flourishing. There was no TV then, and little until the fifties. We wrote letters then, long letters, and instead of channel surfing we read vociferously. We were ambitious to create. Making money was not the objective, it was ancillary. As the years passed, we got older, some of us got married, we had children, and making money acquired a new urgency. But it never was — it never has — become paramount. For being an artist accepted by artists, perhaps appreciated for some impact on the quality of life in our country — beyond our country, our globe — was the goal.

Early in my marriage, my wife and I, along with hundreds of thousands of others, boarded the train from New York to Washington, D.C. and marched against the war in Vietnam. We barely missed being gassed, en route from the Justice Department — put that in quotes — to Union Station.

It is interesting to note that countries step up to the plate in times of darkness and crisis to support and encourage the arts. During the Great Depression, the WPA, the largest federally funded program to date, was founded under FDR's administration. Great Britain's Arts Council was founded after World War I destroyed centuries of priceless art, architecture, and lost manuscripts, and again America responded to the war in Vietnam by establishing both the National Endowments.

In 1965, the National Endowment for the Arts was established to encourage the nourishment of artists and arts organizations. It came at a time when escalating costs and competition from TV were eroding the amount of work we could do in live theater. A huge number of not-for-profit theaters of all sizes and shapes were established across the country, and the average endowment, though small, amounted to imprimaturs in the community. The NEA progressed at a steady pace. I served on the NEA Council of the Arts from 1976 to 1982, and it became obvious during the 1980s that our president did not support the principles of government funding of the arts. Neither did big business. I remember rumors that both endowments, the Arts and the Humanities, were in jeopardy. But thankfully, there was intercession from unexpected quarters. One, a world-renowned movie star reached our Chief of State, and the endowment survived with substantial cutbacks, and the annual budget, which in five years should have grown to a $300+ million-dollar budget, chickenfeed really, was instead cut back from the existing $100 million. In the ensuing years, it has been inching up under the aegis of some excellent public servants, artists in some instances, who've taken up the chairmanship of the NEA.

But, the cynicism hidden behind the specious argument that big corporations would take up the slack created in diminishing budgets still prevails. And what does this mean to us?

That there is diminishing acknowledgment of the place the arts play in our society.

Earlier, I mentioned that in the days of my youth the community was huge and welcoming. Well, the community has shrunken substantially, and with it competition has become more fierce. And the welcome mat is no longer out.

To be fair, there were exciting and positive events fourscore and seven years ago. The League of Women Voters was founded. The America Civil Liberties Union was founded. Mohandas Gandhi staged his first Devotion To Truth crusade. The first United Negro Improvement Association, under the leadership of Marcus Garvey, was established. Women were enfranchised to vote, and 26 million became instantly eligible. Women became 40 percent of all U.S. undergraduates. By the way, the National Football League was established, and in 1920 the world's first radio broadcasting station opened.

It also appears that what goes 'round, comes 'round. However, see how easy it is resisting the impulse to say "those were the good old days," because in truth, they weren't. But these surely are not the good new ones. Remembering our personal March on Washington, I need to ask, what became of all that? Where are the crowds of young people today? Have they sold out to the Great God Mammon? I really don't believe that. Rather,

I believe they've been lulled into blogging each other on the Internet. But visible social activism, believe me, beats blogging every time, and were there a draft, think how different all of this could be. But the powers in charge are smart enough to avoid the draft, and abrogating our duties as citizens is hugely responsible for the state of our union, as we live in it, and as it is perceived by the rest of the world. If we remain inactive, accept the loss of principle, compromise our values, and redefine our responsibilities, our nation, and everything unique and idealistic that it stands for, is perishable.

You have my future in your hands, not just your own. You have the capability to change this world. Time and idealism, talent and energy are on your side. Use them, good luck, and thank you for hearing me out.

Resist!

Wendell Berry

WENDELL BERRY is a renowned poet, essayist, and author of fiction who has written extensively about our need to respect the land. His works of poetry include *New Collected Poems, Given,* and *A Timbered Choir: The Sabbath Poems 1979-1997*; his novels include *A World Lost* and *Remembering*; and his prose collections include *Our Only World: Ten Essays, The Unsettling of America: Culture & Agriculture,* and *Another Turn of the Crank.* He has been a Fellow of the Guggenheim Foundation and the Rockefeller Foundation, and he has also received a Lannan Foundation Award and a grant from the National Endowment for the Arts.

Resist!

Wendell Berry

In his 2007 commencement address at Bellarmine University, Wendell Berry defines a new kind of "resistance" that involves fighting against "the self-destructiveness of our present civilization."

In all the history of teaching and learning, our own time may be the oddest. We seem to be obsessed with education. Newspapers spend an enormous flow of ink on articles, editorials, and letters about education. Presidents of public universities appear on the op-ed pages, prophesying the death of American civilization as the inevitable result of fiscal caution. Our governmental hallways are hardly passable because of university lobbyists kneeling and pleading for public dollars. One might conclude that we are panic-stricken at the thought of any educational inadequacy measurable in unappropriated funds.

And yet by all this fuss we are promoting a debased commodity paid for by the people, sanctioned by the government, for the benefit of the corporations. For the most part, its purpose is now defined by the great and the would-be-great "research universities." These gigantic institutions, increasingly formed upon the "industrial model," no longer make even the pretense of preparing their students for responsible membership in a family, a community, or a polity. They have repudiated their old obligation to pass on to students at least something of their cultural inheritance. The ideal graduate no longer is to have a mind well-equipped to serve others, or to judge competently the purposes for which it may be used.

Now, according to those institutions of the "cutting edge," the purpose of education is unabashedly utilitarian. Their interest is almost exclusively centered in the technical courses called, with typical ostentation of corporate jargon, STEM: science, technology, engineering, and mathematics. The American civilization so ardently promoted by these institutions is to be a civilization entirely determined by technology, and not encumbered by any thought of what is good or worthy or neighborly or humane.

The course of study called STEM is in reality only a sort of job training for upward (and lateral) mobility. It is also a subsidy granted to the corporations, which in a system of free enterprise might reasonably be expected to do their own job training. And in the great universities even this higher job training is obstructed by the hustle and anxiety of "research," often involving yet another corporate raid on the public domain.

I do not mean to say that it is impossible to get something like an education in even the most ambitious university. After all, if you have a library, classrooms, laboratories, and an assemblage of doctors diversely learned, you have the makings of an actual school. And in such a place a young person might still pursue a respectable course of study. But that possibility seems less and less probable.

Actual education seems now to be far more probable in the smaller schools. A school the size of this one can still function as a community of teachers and students, with responsible community life as its unifying aim. But you must not forget that the purposes and standards of the world into which you are graduating have not been set by the smaller institutions such as this one, but rather by the proponents of STEM, who would like you to have a well-paying job as an unconscious expert with Jesus Christ Munitions Incorporated, or Cleanstream Water Polluters, or the Henry Thoreau Noise Factory, or the John Muir Forest Reduction Corporation, or the Promised Land Mountain Removal Service.

You are not going to discover that the STEM project recognizes the standards of ecological and community health, or that it proposes the real national security of coherent local economies or sustainable methods of land use. You will be told instead that you and your community are now ruled by a global corporate empire to which all the earth is a "third world," against which you have no power of resistance or self-determination, and within which you have no vocational choice except a technical and servile job, which will give you a small share of the plunder.

You will be told also — ignoring our permanent dependence on food, clothing, and shelter — that you live in a "knowledge-based economy," which in fact is deeply prejudiced against all knowledge that does not produce the quickest possible return on investment. Even as the ecologists (who manifestly are excluded from STEM) have greatly enlarged our knowledge of ecosystems, their complexity and fragility and their need for care, our knowledge of our own species has been radically simplified. STEM's definition of humanity includes no suggestion of reverence or neighborliness or stewardship. Instead, people are encouraged to think of themselves as individuals, self-interested and greedy by nature, violent by economic predestination, and members of nothing except their careers. The lives of these "autonomous" individuals will be "successful" insofar as they subserve the purposes of the corporate-political powers, who will regard them merely as consumers, votes, and units of "human capital."

At commencement exercises it is customary to invite a speaker to exhort the graduates not to think of the end of their formal education as the end of their education, but rather to continue to learn and to grow in consciousness as they go forth to the duties and trials of responsible citizenship. As the designated speaker of this ceremony, I am serious about this duty. I do hereby exhort the graduates to continue to learn and to grow in consciousness as responsible citizens. And I do so knowing that no exhortation could be more subversive in the world as defined by the proponents of STEM.

To urge you toward responsible citizenship is to say that I do not accept either the technological determinism or the conventional greed or the thoughtless individualism of that world. Nor do I accept the global corporate empire and its economic totalitarianism as an irresistible force. I am here to say that if you love your family, your neighbors, your community, and your place, you are going to have to resist. Or I should say instead that you are going to have to join the many others, all over our country and the world, who already are resisting — those who believe, in spite of the obstacles and the odds, that a reasonable measure of self-determination, for persons and communities, is both desirable and necessary. Of the possibility of effective resistance there is a large, ever-growing catalogue of proofs: of projects undertaken by local people, without official permission or instruction, that *work* to reduce the toxicity, the violence, and the self-destructiveness of our present civilization.

The resistance I am recommending will involve you endlessly in out-of-school learning, the curriculum of which will be defined by questions such as these: What more than you have so far learned will you need to know in order to live at home? (I don't mean "home" as a house for sale.) If you decide, or if you are required by circumstances, to live all your life in one place, what will you need to know about that place and about yourself? At present our economy and society are founded on the assumption that energy will always be unlimited and cheap; but what will you have to learn in order to live in a world in which energy is limited and expensive? What will you have to know — and know how to do — when your community can no longer be supplied by cheap transportation? Will you be satisfied to live in a world owned or controlled by a few great corporations? If not, would you consider the alternative: self-employment in a small local enterprise owned by you, offering honest goods or services to your neighbors and responsible stewardship to your place and community?

Even to ask such questions, let alone answer them, you will have to refuse certain assumptions that the proponents of STEM and the predestinarians of the global economy wish you to take for granted.

You will have to avoid thinking of yourselves as employable minds equipped with a few digits useful for pushing buttons. You will have to recover for yourselves the old understanding that you are whole beings inextricably and mysteriously compounded of minds and bodies.

You will have to understand that the logic of success is radically different from the logic of vocation. The logic of what our society means by "success" supposedly leads you ever upward to any higher-paying job that can be done sitting down. The logic of vocation holds that there is an indispensable justice, to yourself and to others, in doing well the work that you are "called" or prepared by your talents to do.

And so you must refuse to accept the common delusion that a career is an adequate context for a life. The logic of success insinuates that self-enlargement is your only responsibility, and that any job, any career will be satisfying if you succeed in it. But I can tell you, on the authority of much evidence, that a lot of people highly successful by that logic are painfully dissatisfied. I can tell you further that you cannot live in a career, and that satisfaction can come only from your life. To give satisfaction, your life will have to be lived in a family, a neighborhood, a community, an ecosystem, a watershed, a *place*, meeting your responsibilities to all those things to which you belong.

I am sure that you are going to come face to face with the questions and issues I have mentioned, and I am sure that I don't know how you will answer. People who speak at commencements speak in hope, but also in ignorance. However you may answer, I join the rest of your elders in worrying about you and in wishing you well.

High Stakes

David Levering Lewis

DAVID LEVERING LEWIS is a noted historian and is the first author to win two consecutive Pulitzer Prizes — for his celebrated two-part biography of W. E. B. Du Bois. He is also the author of *God's Crucible* and *When Harlem Was in Vogue*. Dr. Lewis is Professor, Emeritus, in the New York University History Department. He is the recipient of the Bancroft Prize and the Francis Parkman Prize and has received fellowships from the Center for Advanced Study in the Behavioral Sciences, the National Endowment for the Humanities, the Woodrow Wilson International Center for Scholars, the John Simon Guggenheim Foundation, and a five-year John D. and Catherine T. MacArthur Foundation Fellowship. He is a past president of the Society of American Historians; a board member of *The Crisis* magazine, published by the NAACP; and a Fellow of the American Academy of Arts and Sciences.

High Stakes

David Levering Lewis

In his 2004 commencement address at Bates College, David Levering Lewis recounts the prescient words of W. E. B. Du Bois, who wrote in his own time of how a "wave of materialism . . . strangely maddens and blinds us."

You are going out into an America whose constant self-reinvention was acknowledged this past week in celebration and contemplation of the fiftieth anniversary of *Brown v. Board of Education*. You are going to work, play, bond, vote, and parent in a multi-cultural nation of accelerating ethnic, demographic, gendered, and politico-economic complexity. It is a nation that has come about in major measure because of the ongoing revolution in civil rights whose momentum has propelled women, ethnics, gays, and other challenged categories that continue to emerge and lay claim to a fair share of the vaunted American Dream. For nothing could be more obvious to us now than that the civil rights struggle of African Americans commenced the fight for the optimal expansion of everybody's rights.

To be sure, the considerable social gains of the last fifty years are only as authentic and as enduring as your vigilant guardianship will make them. I hardly need tell you that you have your work cut out for you. Your generation is facing not only concerted assaults through the federal courts upon minority advancement in secondary and higher education and women's reproductive rights, you and we confront the most formidable, and related, assault upon the very possibility of economic and political democracy in this country since the late 1890s.

As the biographer of one of this nation's most extraordinary public intellectuals, I'm frequently challenged to speculate on what W.E.B. Du Bois would say about these times. Mostly, I resist such requests as an exercise in improper historical license. Nevertheless, the temptation to speak to you through his salient, prescient words is, on occasions such as this, irresistible. One hundred years ago in William Randolph Hearst's *World Today*, Du Bois deplored his times in accents of exceptional pertinence to our times: "The gospel of money has been triumphant in church and state and university. The great question which Americans ask today is, 'What is he worth?' or 'What is it worth?' The ideals of human rights are obscured and the nation has begun to swagger about the world in useless battleships looking for helpless peoples whom it can force to buy its goods at high prices. This wave of materialism is temporary; it will pass and leave us all ashamed and surprised; but while it is here it strangely maddens and blinds us."

I doubt that most of us here feel much confidence that what the thirty-six-year-old Du Bois called a temporary "wave of materialism" is in reality a passing phenomenon. Du Bois himself realized at the end of the day that the fundamental problem of his twentieth and our twenty-first century was not solely the famous color line but unregulated economic greed: the exploitation of the great majority of humankind by the kleptocratic minority. Who among us here doesn't know that since the 1980s, the maldistribution of income in the United States has become greater in favor of the rich than in any other modern democracy and is rapidly growing worse? More to the point, there are few real jobs in an economy where money chases after money, and business mergers produce watered stock and a contracting labor market in which real goods are produced mostly anywhere but here. Much of higher education is now priced so far above the means of middle-class Americans as to be available, if at all, only through crushing indebtedness. In 2004, the political ethos in which taxes for social-democratic initiatives can be meaningfully debated no longer exists.

As for that swaggering about the world that Du Bois deplored, that too appears to be with us indefinitely. 9/11 has robbed us once again of that innocence we Americans lose every other decade. Quite understandably, many of us feel that we have to trade some of our liberties in return for our security. This is an old, bad Faustian bargain. Unless we take great care, the Homeland Security State and its Justice Department handmaidens, Patriots Act I and II, may well leave our civil liberties as maimed as the New York cityscape has been by the al-Qaeda jihadists. The damage done to the United States in the community of nations through the perverse logic of superpower omnipotence affronts those fine Wilsonian principles much of the world is now beginning to try to abide by. To many of us, this fastening on of domestic vigilantism and international hooliganism is thought to be the consequence of international terrorism — an aberration running against the grain of American history. Yesterday, we had a republic, they say. Today we have the Homeland Security State. How can all this have happened? The reality, of course, is that there has always been an American counter-narrative that trumps the narratives of Walt Whitman and Woodrow Wilson. There has always been a dark side to that mythic city on a hill whence our ideal and institutions are said to derive. From this day forward, you are going to be challenged to be more discerning about the values that matter than any college generation since Vietnam. In this regard, I think of no more apt observation than one made by an illustrious Bates alumnus, who said: "I would rather go to hell by choice than to stumble into heaven by following the crowd." These words were spoken by Benjamin Mays, Phi Beta Kappa, Class of 1920.

If I've learned anything from my profession, it is that the future is never certain until it becomes history. It is fitting to expect you to play a significant part in the writing of the American future and to help determine, thereby, whether you will be citizens of an American Empire that mimics imperial Rome or of a republic dedicated to the planetary spread of knowledge, science, and technology through democracy. Perhaps, as Winston Churchill famously opined, "Americans will always do the right thing — after trying all the other alternatives." Regardless of the fears and challenges, the good news today is that you are uniquely equipped for leadership. I envy your options, because they really are breathtakingly historic. And now it's up to you to make history come out the right way.

The Creepy Biological Facts of Life

Tess Gerritsen

Tess Gerritsen, the author of award-winning international best sellers, first began to write fiction while on maternity leave from her work as a physician. Among her twenty-six suspense novels are *The Surgeon*, *The Bone Garden*, *Gravity*, *Vanish*, and *Die Again*, and her crime series featuring Detective Jane Rizzoli and Dr. Maura Isles inspired the television series *Rizzoli & Isles*. Her novels have been translated into forty languages and more than thirty million copies have been sold around the world.

The Creepy Biological Facts of Life

Tess Gerritsen

In her 2007 commencement address at the University of Maine, Tess Gerritsen presents five "creepy facts" that have valuable life lessons for us all.

I grew up in a world of ghosts. My mother is an immigrant from China, and she believed in a supernatural world of spirits and demons, a world where magical things could happen. She also had a great love of horror films, and she would bring my brother and me to every scary movie that came to our local theater. I spent much of my childhood screaming at the movies. Horror movies taught me that when you turn over a rock, something terrifying would probably crawl out. If you unlocked a forbidden door, you'd almost certainly find a monster on the other side. Eventually, though, I became a skeptic of all things supernatural. I studied science and became a physician. But I have never lost my appreciation for the bizarre and the creepy — in particular, the creepy aspects of science. Over the years, I've collected a file of weird scientific facts, facts that remind us that Mother Nature is one very scary lady. In the natural world of thrills and chills, you will find most of the lessons you'll ever need to navigate through life. I now present you with some items from my file of creepy facts, and I hope you'll find them relevant to your own lives.

Creepy Fact #1: In the Amazon, there is a species of tiny catfish known as the candiru. It's an inch long, translucent, and needle thin, so it's almost invisible to the human eye. Like other catfish, it has razor-sharp dorsal spines, which it can extend or fold back at will. It lives a parasitic existence burrowed in the gills of other fish, and it finds its way to its host by following the scent of urea. Now let's say you are a man who decides to take a swim in the Amazon River. And while you're swimming, you feel the inconvenient need to empty your bladder. You're underwater anyway, so you pee. The little candiru fish smells the urea in your urine and follows it back toward its source. Once it finds itself in a nice, warm, cozy little passage, it extends its spines and lodges there, most obstinately, causing its human host to react with blood-curdling screams of a most unmanly nature. A case of urethral candiru is one of the rare conditions in which the patient may beg for a penile amputation.

Now, what's the lesson this little catfish can teach us about life? First, be careful where you swim. If you swim with sharks or piranhas, you know what might happen. You know you can't trust them. Likewise, don't swim with sneaky little fish that may stab you with their razor-sharp spines when you're not looking. Don't hang out with these creatures at all, no matter how alluring or seductive they may seem. Certainly don't marry them. You're old enough to know which sort of people I'm talking about. Choose good friends who will last, friends you can trust. And likewise, be a true friend to them.

The second lesson the candiru fish can teach us is this: Be careful where you take a piss. Don't foul the water where you live. Don't poison your workplace with gossip. I work in the publishing industry, and if I were to say nasty things about an editor or agent or another writer behind her back, you can pretty much bet she will eventually hear it. It's the same for any other business out there. The people you piss on today will never forget it. And the chances are, you will meet them again.

Creepy Fact #2: Decades ago, an epidemic of a bizarre disease called kuru broke out in a tribe in New Guinea. Victims began to laugh weirdly, and then hallucinate. Soon their muscles were jerking, they had seizures, and invariably, they died. What puzzled doctors was the fact that the victims were almost entirely women or children — men were not affected. So many women were dying of it that there were twice as many men alive as women in this tribe. No one could explain why. The doctors worked with the blood tests and the brain biopsies and they had a thorough knowledge of medicine. But they didn't know enough beyond their immediate sphere of expertise. What was killing the women of this tribe? Only when the anthropologists arrived and began asking the right questions, the cultural questions, was the mystery solved. What the anthropologists discovered was that the women were doing a very secret thing that the men were not. The women were eating their dead relatives. When a loved one died, the women performed a grief ritual that involved taking the corpse into the potato fields and cooking the body. Then the women would consume the brains. As a result, they caught the disease kuru. They would die, and be eaten, and more women would catch it.

The obvious lesson to be learned from this creepy fact is that you shouldn't eat your dead relatives. But there's also another lesson, and it's this: When you're trying to solve a problem, it's important to ask the right question. But it takes a certain amount of basic knowledge to know what that right question might be. Those doctors knew all about medicine, but they didn't know enough about anthropology. They couldn't come up with the right questions.

In your own lives, you are going to face dilemmas, in the workplace or in the voting booth. You will have to make some educated decisions. How will you know what questions to ask? You can start now, by becoming an information pack rat. A collector of knowledge. You never know when some obscure fact you learn today will be vital to you ten years from now. If you want to collect facts, you have to be exposed to them, and you won't get them from watching *American Idol.*

From this day forward, every single day of your life, you must read a newspaper. It can be any newspaper, as long as it covers both national and international news. Maybe you think a subscription is too expensive at this stage in your lives. Your parents can give you a gift: a subscription to the *Bangor Daily News* or the *Boston Globe* or the *New York Times.* Don't just read the sports page and throw out the rest. No, you should read, from front to back, at least the A section of the newspaper. Force yourself. For the first few weeks, it might feel like a slog. Does anyone really care about Ahmadinejad or Sarkozy or Vladimir Putin? But over time, as you read, you'll become familiar with all these names. You'll begin to realize that what happens in Cairo or Beijing could very well affect you. You'll see that the world is far more complicated than you imagined and that actions can have unintended consequences. Before you send troops into harm's way, at least you'll be educated enough to ask the question: What's the difference between a Shiite and a Sunni, and does it matter?

Creepy Fact #3: In a certain valley in Kentucky, people were coming down with a strange disease. It was affecting both young and old alike, and it appeared that they were all suffering from a form of mad cow disease. Except it wasn't from cows — it was from squirrels. These people were dying from mad squirrel disease. In that region of Kentucky, it seems that a favorite snack among the locals is squirrel brains. When you'd visit a friend up the valley, to be neighborly, you'd bring along a sack of squirrel heads. Your hostess would fry those heads up in a cast-iron skillet, and then you'd sit around the table cracking the skulls and sucking out the tender little brains. Yum. But as we just learned from the epidemic of kuru in New Guinea, eating brains is not a very wise thing to do.

The first lesson to be learned here is culinary: Be selective about what you put in your mouths. I'm the daughter of a restaurant chef, and one thing my dad taught me was this: You can enjoy only so many meals in a lifetime. Try to make each one worthwhile. Forget margarine and just go for butter. Eat less, but let each bite be exquisite. Avoid squirrel brains.

There's a corollary lesson as well, and it's not about food. Be critical about what you consume from the media. Because what you put into your brain is as important as what you put into your mouth. Whether food or information, insist on the truth. Don't swallow propaganda, even though it's quick and easy to digest, the equivalent of those fast-food outlets we see on the highways. The truth is often a lot more complicated, but like real food, worthwhile food, in the end, it's a lot more satisfying.

Creepy Fact #4: Things that look dead really can come back to life. This is from a news article I read a few years ago in the *Boston Globe*. The story is this: In a suburb outside Boston, a young woman was discovered dead in her bathtub. The state police were called and they found empty pill bottles beside her. They assumed that her death was due to an accidental overdose, so they zipped her into a body bag and sent her to the morgue. Where, a few hours later, she woke up. As it turns out, being mistaken for dead is not all that rare a phenomenon. I did a news search on LexisNexis and discovered case after case of it. In Colorado, a child's death certificate had just been signed when someone noticed he was breathing. In Georgia, a young man who'd been hit by a car spent a whole night in the morgue refrigerator before someone heard him moving. In New York City, a man was lying on the autopsy table and the pathologist was about to make the first cut when the corpse woke up and grabbed the doctor. It was the doctor who keeled over dead, of a heart attack.

There is a lesson to be learned in these premature declarations of death. And the lesson is: yes, sometimes, you do get a second chance at life. Sometimes you really can live twice.

Back when dinosaurs roamed the earth, and I was a college student in California, I shared a house off-campus with four other students in the town of Palo Alto. A student named Sally used to stop by pretty regularly, because she played tennis with one of my housemates. Sally was a great tennis player. All through her childhood, her dream was to play professional tennis. She won scholarships and regional championships. She was so good at tennis that she dropped out of college and turned pro. But after three months on the professional tennis circuit, she came to a sad realization: she would never be good enough to reach the top.

For nearly ten years, Sally had pursued a dream, only to discover that her dream was unattainable. She felt devastated. Her future as a star was over.

But this is not a story about failure. Let's find out what happened next to Sally.

Realizing that she had to make a course correction in her life, she went back to college, enrolling at Stanford University, and chose to study physics. That's how I knew her — as "Sally in the physics program." At twenty-seven, while she was a

Ph.D. candidate, looking for a job in astrophysics, she read that NASA was looking for astronauts. She applied, and out of eight thousand applicants, thirty-five were accepted. Sally was one of them.

In 1983, Dr. Sally Ride became the first American woman to be launched into outer space. She flew on two shuttle missions, and in 1986 was preparing for her third when the shuttle Challenger exploded. In the terrible aftermath of that tragedy, she was appointed to the commission charged with investigating the accident. Disillusioned by what she learned, she left NASA.

You may think that this is the end of the story. That Sally had her moment of glory and faded off into the sunset, a has-been.

In 1989, Sally went on to become Professor of Physics at the University of California. She became president of Space.com, a space industry Web site. She's written five books and founded the company Sally Ride Science, which designs science education programs. At the age of fifty-six, she's been a tennis player, an astronaut, a university professor, an author, and a business CEO. Not to mention an American hero.

She's the perfect example of someone who, at different stages in her life, failed, and thought her career was finished. Then she picked herself up, and moved on to bigger and better things. She saw the need for change and made the change — in her case, several times over.

I have another story, about a boy I went to high school with. His name is Randy. After high school he graduated from West Point and went on to travel the world, representing a defense company. It sounds like a cool job, but at the age of thirty-five, Randy hated it. What he'd always wanted to be was a writer, and he had one particular dream: he wanted to write for Hollywood. The problem was, he was living in Seattle. Still, he took a chance. He saved up enough money to leave his job and moved to Los Angeles. He gave himself one year to make it. Within three months, he landed a job as a TV writer at Warner Brothers. Two years later, he received his first Emmy Award and was working for Steven Spielberg.

Maybe you're thinking: These stories are totally irrelevant to my life. I can't worry about how I'm going to feel when I'm thirty-five. Some of you already know exactly what you want to do with your lives. You've hit on the perfect career, you'll stick with it, and it will give you a lifetime of satisfaction. To those lucky people, I say, good for you. May reality match your dreams.

But life can change, in ways you can't predict. What you thought was a dream job turns out to be a daily ordeal. Or you get fired. Or your business collapses. You'll wake up at age thirty or forty or fifty (some of you parents may be going through this right now) and suddenly realize that you hate your job, and you desperately want to do something different. You want another chance. You want another life. I'm here to tell you that it's not impossible.

The chance to have a second career is a relatively new thing in human history. Back in the days of the Roman Empire, the human lifespan was twenty-two years. If you were living back then, most of you wouldn't be graduating today. You'd be dead. With a lifespan of only twenty-two, you'd be lucky just to reproduce. You wouldn't live long enough to have a second career. You'd work hard and you'd die young.

But today, an American newborn can expect to live to the age of seventy-six. That's three times longer than people lived in Ancient Rome. The odds are, you have at least fifty years ahead of you. You have a chance for not just one life, but two or three.

Someday in the future, you may wake up and think: *I want a second chance.* And you'll remember that some lady years before told you that something like this might happen. But you were too busy thinking about other things so you weren't really listening. What was her advice again?

Here it is:

If you have a dream, learn what you need to know to make it happen. Randy and Sally are, I admit, exceptional examples. Not everyone can take a risk and find success. Not everyone's in a position to take risks. Some people, when told to "follow your heart," end up broke, unhappy, and worse off. Lots of people dream about being screenwriters, but when my friend Randy decided that was his goal, he didn't just sit around talking about the movie he was going to write someday. He studied scripts. He wrote them. He sent them out to Hollywood agents. He saved up enough money to tide him over for a lean year in Los Angeles. He arrived with a list of agents to contact, with a bundle of sample scripts he'd already written. He didn't sit and dream; he worked hard to perfect his craft.

When I decided I wanted to be a novelist, I didn't just talk about writing. I did it. I was working as a doctor at the time, so I wrote in the on-call room, I wrote on my lunch break, I wrote late at night after my kids were put to bed. And I read novels — lots and lots of them, to learn how other writers do it. Occasionally, now, I'll teach courses about writing, and it always astonishes me when I encounter students who tell me they dream of being novelists but they just can't find the time to write. Or even worse, they don't have the time to read. When I hear that, I want to tell them: Just give up now, because you aren't a writer. You'll never be a writer. You're just a dreamer. And dreams don't come true all by themselves.

Finally, I leave you to ponder **Creepy Fact #5:** The animal with the shortest lifespan is the aquatic gastrotrich. It lives only three days. Only three days to accomplish everything it needs to do in a lifetime.

You, on the other hand, have fifty years ahead of you. That may seem like a long time right now, but it isn't. I'm a gardener, and we gardeners know that we're allotted only a limited number of spring plantings in our lives, only a certain number of seasons to try out new plants. So here's the final lesson from my creepy facts file, a lesson brought to you courtesy of the pitifully short-lived gastrotrich: Don't waste a single planting season. Plant the seeds of your future now by nurturing every interest, every hobby. And always have something new growing, something you've never tried to grow before. Because you never know. It could end up being the most beautiful plant in your garden.

Now go out and start planting.

Be Not Afraid

Anna Quindlen

ANNA QUINDLEN is an acclaimed author whose books have appeared on the fiction, nonfiction, and self-help best-seller lists of the *New York Times*. She won the Pulitzer Prize for her commentary in the *New York Times*, and her novels include *Still Life with Bread Crumbs*; *Rise and Shine*; *Black and Blue* (an Oprah Book Club selection); and *One True Thing*; and her nonfiction includes *Lots of Candles, Plenty of Cake*; *Good Dog, Stay*; *Being Perfect*; and *A Short Guide to a Happy Life*.

Be Not Afraid

Anna Quindlen

In her 2006 commencement address at Colby College, Anna Quindlen reveals how to perform "the ultimate act of bravery."

Commencement speeches are the toughest speeches I ever give. This is a hugely transformative moment in the life of you graduates and of all of your families. It's also a day of great celebration, and I'm always keenly aware that I am now all that stands between you and your diplomas and the partying to come. So I'm going to be brief with you. My text is a simple one — you can remember it.

Be not afraid.

It's an old and honorable directive — you can find it with some variation in both the Old and the New Testament. That's because it's really the secret of life. C.S. Lewis once wrote, "Courage is not simply one of the virtues, but the form of every virtue at the testing point." So, Class of 2006, fear not.

Believe me, I have enough of a memory of my youth to know that it's really preposterous to say that at this moment. You are afraid. You're afraid of leaving what you know, you're afraid of seeking what you want, you're afraid of taking the wrong path, or you're afraid of failing at the right one. Your closest friends are going one way, you're going another, and from this small, serene, safe, gorgeous pond, you go down through the estuary to the ocean, and often the current will be harsh and the riptides will be tough. But you have to learn to put the fear aside, or at least refuse to allow it to rule you.

It is fear that always tamps down our authentic selves, that turns us into some patchwork collection of affectations and expectations, mores and mannerisms, some treadmill set to the prevailing speed of universal acceptability that causes a tyranny of homogeny, whether it's the homogeny of the straight world of the suits or the spiky world of the avant-garde.

The voices of conformity speak so loudly out there. Don't listen. People will tell you what you ought to think and how you ought to feel. They will tell you what to read and how to live. They will urge you to take jobs that they themselves loathe, and to follow safe paths that they themselves find tedious.

Only a principled refusal to be terrorized by these stingy standards will save you from a Frankenstein life that's made up of others' outside expectations grafted together into a poor semblance of existence.

You can't afford to do that. It's what's poisoned our culture, our communities, and our national character. No one ever does the right thing from fear, and so many of the wrong things are done in its shadow: homophobia, sexism, racism, religious bigotry. All of them are bricks in a wall that divides us and they're bricks cast of the clay of fear — fear of that which is different or unknown.

Our political atmosphere today is so dispiriting because most of our leaders are leaders in name only. They're terrorized by polls and focus groups, by the need to be all things to all people, which means that they wind up being nothing at all.

Our workplaces are full of fear — fear of innovation, fear of difference. The most widely used cliché in management today is to "think outside the box." The box is not only stale custom, it is terrified paralysis.

In my own business fear is the ultimate enemy. It accounts for censorship, obfuscation, the lowest common denominator of the news when sharp, free, fearless news is more necessary to us than ever before. Without fear or favor, the news business has to provide readers and viewers with stories, even if those stories are stories the powerful do not want you to hear or believe and do not want us to publish or disseminate.

Too often our public discourse fears real engagement or intellectual intercourse. It pitches itself at the lowest possible level. Always preaching to the choir so that nobody will get angry, which means nobody will get interested. What's the point of free speech if we're always afraid to speak freely?

Not too long ago I asked a professor of religion what she did to suit the comfort level of all those diverse students in her class. And she said, "It's not my job to make people comfortable. It's my job to *educate* them." I nearly stood up and cheered.

If we fear competing viewpoints, in this country of *all* countries, if we fail to state the unpopular or to allow the unacceptable to be heard because of some plain-vanilla sense of civility, that's not civility at all, it's the denigration of the human capacity for thought — the suggestion that we are fragile flowers incapable of disagreement, argument, or civil intellectual combat.

Colby College does not turn out fragile flowers. You have to be smart and sure and strong enough to overcome the condescending notion that opposing viewpoints are just too much for us to bear — in politics, in journalism, in business, in the academy. Open your mouths. Speak your peace. Fear not.

Believe me, you're not the only ones who sometimes lack courage. We parents have been paralyzed by fear as well, haven't we? When you were first born, each of you, I can guarantee that your parents' greatest glory was in thinking you absolutely distinct from every baby who had ever been born before. You were a miracle of singularity. You shouted "dog," you lurched across the playground, you put a scrawl of red paint next to a squiggle of green and we put it on the fridge and said, "Oh my god, oh my god, you are a painter, a poet, a prodigy, a genius."

But we are only human, and being a parent is a very difficult job — unpaid and unrewarded much of the time, requiring the shaping of other people — an act of incredible hubris. And over the years, we sometimes learned to want for you things that you did not necessarily want for yourselves. We learned to want the lead in the play, the acceptance at our own college, the straight and narrow path that often leads absolutely nowhere. We learned to fear your differences, not to celebrate them.

Sometimes we were convinced conformity would make life better or at least easier for you. Sometimes we had a hard time figuring out where we ended and you began.

So today guide us back to where we started. Help us not to

make mistakes out of fear, or out of love. Learn not to listen to us when we are wrong. Begin today to say no to the Greek chorus that thinks it knows the parameters of a good life when all it knows is some one-size-fits-all version of human experience.

There's plenty to fear out there. You know that every time you pick up a newspaper. Two years ago I gave into it myself, writing a column at just this time called "An Apology to the Graduates," telling the Class of 2004 how sorry I was about the unremitting stress they had been under all their young lives. In part I wrote, "There's an honorable tradition of starving students; it's just that between outsourcing of jobs and a boom market in real estate, your generation envisions becoming starving adults. Caught in our peculiar modern nexus of prosperity and insolvency, easy credit and epidemic bankruptcy, you also get toxic messages from the culture about what achievement means. It is no longer enough to make it, you must make it big. You all will live longer than any generation in history, yet you were kicked into high gear earlier as well. Your college applications look like the résumés for midlevel executives. How exhausted you must be."

Well, here is what might await you. You will, I am sure, be offered the option of now becoming exhausted adults, convinced that no achievement is large enough, with résumés as long as short stories. But what if that feels like a betrayal of your true self? A forced march down a road trodden by other feet at the end of which is nothing you truly care for?

Fear not. Remember Pinocchio? Each of you has a Jiminy Cricket. It is you, your best self, the one you can trust. The only problem is that it is sometimes hard to hear what it says because all of the external voices and messages are so loud, so insistent, and so adamant.

Voices that loud are always meant to bully. Do not be bullied. You already know this. I just need to remind you. You already know how important courage is. After all, you chose as your class speaker someone from a small village in Zimbabwe who got on a plane to transcend hemispheres, customs, and cultures to come to Colby College. You can look at him and know that a flying leap of fearlessness is possible.

Just think back. You know how to do this. Think back to first grade — to yourself in first grade when you could still hear the sound of your own voice in your head. When you were too young, too unformed, too fantastic to understand that you were supposed to take on the protective coloration of the expectations of those around you. When you were absolutely, certainly, unapologetically yourself.

I have a pocket-sized edition of the Tao that I keep on my desk. I read a passage from it every day, and the section I like best says, "In dwelling, live close to the ground. In thinking, keep to the simple. In conflict, be fair and generous. In governing, don't try to control. In work, do what you enjoy. In family life, be completely present."

When you are content to be simply yourself and don't compare or compete, everybody will respect you.

We live in a world in which the simple, the generous, the enjoyable, the completely present, above all the simply yourself, sometimes seems as out of reach as the moon. Don't be fooled. That's not because anyone has found a better way in the millennia since the Tao was written. It is because too often we are people enslaved by fear.

The ultimate act of bravery doesn't usually take place on a battlefield. It takes place in your heart when you have the courage to honor your character, your intellect, your inclinations, and your soul by listening to its clean, clear voice of direction instead of following the muddied messages of a timid world.

Samuel Butler once said, "Life is likc playing a violin solo in public and learning the instrument as one goes on." That sounds terrifying, doesn't it, and difficult too, but that way lies music. So, Class of 2006, pick up your violin, lift your bow, play your heart out.

Congratulations and courage.

Let Us Commence

Anne Lamott

ANNE LAMOTT is the author of the *New York Times* best sellers *Small Victories*; *Help, Thanks, Wow*; *Some Assembly Required*; *Grace (Eventually)*; *Plan B*; and several others. A past recipient of a Guggenheim Fellowship and an inductee to the California Hall of Fame, she lives in Northern California.

Let Us Commence

Anne Lamott

In her 2003 commencement address at the University of California at Berkeley, Anne Lamott shares her unique perspectives on the value of "Prone Yoga," the perils of "uncomfortable pants," and why you need to "refuse to cooperate with anyone who is trying to shame you into hopping right back up onto the rat exercise wheel."

I am honored and surprised that you asked me to speak today.

This must be a magical day for you. I wouldn't know. I accidentally forgot to graduate from college. I meant to, thirty years ago, but things got away from me. I did graduate from high school, though — do I get a partial credit for that? Although, unfortunately, my father had forgotten to pay the book bill, so at the graduation ceremony, when I opened the case to see my diploma, it was empty. Except for a ransom note that said, see Mrs. Foley, the bookkeeper, if you ever want to see your diploma alive again.

I went to Goucher College in Maryland for the best possible reasons — to learn — but then I dropped out at nineteen for the best possible reasons — to become a writer. Those of you who have read my work know that instead, I accidentally became a Kelly girl for a while. Then, in a dazzling career move, I got hired as a clerk typist in the Nuclear Quality Assurance Department at Bechtel, where I worked typing and sorting triplicate forms. I hate to complain, but it was not very stimulating work. But it paid the bills, so I could write my stories every night when I got home. I worked at Bechtel for six months — but I had nothing to do with the current administration's shameless war profiteering. I just sorted triplicate forms. You've got to believe me.

It was a terrible job, at which I did a terrible job, but it paid $600 a month, which was enough to pay my rent and bills. This is the real fly in the ointment if you are crazy enough to want to be an artist — you have to give up your dreams of swimming pools and fish forks, and take any old job. At twenty, I got hired at a magazine as an assistant editor, and I think that was the last real job I've ever had.

I bet I'm beginning to make your parents really nervous — here I am sort of bragging about being a dropout, and unemployable, and secretly making a pitch for you to follow your creative dreams, when what they want is for you to do well in your field, make them look good, and maybe also make a tiny fortune.

But that is not your problem. Your problem is how you are going to spend this one odd and precious life you have been issued. Whether you're going to spend it trying to look good and creating the illusion that you have power over people and circumstances, or whether you are going to taste it, enjoy it, and find out the truth about who you are.

At some point I finally started getting published, and experiencing a meager knock-kneed standing in the literary world, and I started to get almost everything that many of you graduates are hoping for — except for the money.

I got a lot of things that society had promised would make me whole and fulfilled — all the things that the culture tells you from preschool on will quiet the throbbing anxiety inside you — stature, the respect of colleagues, maybe even a kind of low-grade fame. The culture says these things will save you, as long as you also manage to keep your weight down. But the culture lies.

Slowly, after dozens of rejection slips and failures and false starts and postponed dreams — what Langston Hughes called dreams deferred — I stepped onto the hallowed ground of being a published novelist, and then fifteen years later, I even started to make real money.

I'd been wanting to be a successful author my whole life. But when I finally did it, I was like a greyhound catching the mechanical rabbit she'd been chasing all her life — metal, wrapped up in cloth. It wasn't alive; it had no spirit. It was fake. Fake doesn't feed anything. Only spirit feeds spirit, in the same way only your own blood type can sustain you. It had nothing that could slake the lifelong thirst I had for a little immediacy, and connection.

So from the wise old pinnacle of my forty-nine years, I want to tell you that what you're looking for is already inside you. You've heard this before, but the holy thing inside you really is that which causes you to seek it. You can't buy it, lease it, rent it, date it or apply for it. The best job in the world can't give it to you. Neither can success, or fame, or financial security — besides which, there ain't no such thing. J.D. Rockefeller was asked, "How much money is enough?" and he said, "Just a little bit more."

So it can be confusing — most of your parents want you to do well, to be successful. They want you to be happy — or at least happy-ish. And they want you to be *nicer* to them; just a little nicer — is that so much to ask?

They want you to love, and be loved, and to find peace, and to laugh and find meaningful work. But they also — some of them — a few of them — not yours — yours are fine — they also want you to chase the bunny for a while. To get ahead, sock some away, and then find a balance between the greyhound bunny-chase, and savoring your life.

But the thing is that you don't know if you're going to live long enough to slow down, relax, and have fun, and discover the truth of your spiritual identity. You may not be destined to live a long life; you may not have sixty more years to discover and claim your own deepest truth — like Breaker Morant said, you have to live every day as if it's your last, because one of these days, you're bound to be right.

So I thought it might help if I just went ahead and told you what I think is the truth of your spiritual identity...

Actually, I don't have a clue.

I do know you are not what you look like, or how much you weigh, or how you did in school, and whether you get to start a job next Monday or not. Spirit isn't what you do, it's ... well, again, I don't actually know. They probably taught this junior year at Goucher. But I know that you feel it best when you're not doing much — when you're in nature, when you're very quiet, or, paradoxically, listening to music.

I know you can feel it and hear it in the music you love, in the bass line, in the harmonies, in the silence between notes; in Chopin and Eminem, Emmylou Harris, Bach, whoever. You can close your eyes and feel the divine spark, concentrated in you, like a little Dr. Seuss firefly. It flickers with aliveness and relief, like an American in a foreign country who suddenly hears someone speaking in English. In the Christian tradition, they say that the soul rejoices in hearing what it already knows. And so you pay attention when that Dr. Seuss creature inside you sits up and says, "Yo!"

We can see spirit made visible in people being kind to each other, especially when it's a really busy person, taking care of a needy annoying person. Or even if it's terribly important you, stopping to take care of pitiful, pathetic you. In fact, that's often when we see spirit most brightly.

It's magic to see spirit largely because it's so rare. Mostly you see the masks and the holograms that the culture presents as real. You see how you're doing in the world's eyes, or your family's, or — worst of all — yours, or in the eyes of people who are doing better than you — much better than you — or worse. But you are not your bank account, or your ambitiousness. You're not the cold clay lump with a big belly you leave behind when you die. You're not your collection of walking personality disorders. You are spirit, you are love, and, while it is increasingly hard to believe during this presidency, you are free. You're here to love, and be loved, freely. If you find out next week that you are terminally ill — and we're all terminally ill on this bus — all that will matter is memories of beauty, that people loved you, and you loved them, and that you tried to help the poor and innocent.

So how do we feed and nourish our spirit, and the spirit of others?

First, find a path, and a little light to see by. Every single spiritual tradition says the same three things: 1) Live in the now, as often as you can, a breath here, a moment there. 2) You reap exactly what you sow. 3) You must take care of the poor, or you are so doomed that we can't help you.

You don't have to go overseas. There are people right here who are poor in spirit; worried, depressed, dancing as fast as they can, whose kids are sick, or whose retirement savings are gone. There is great loneliness among us, life-threatening loneliness. People have given up on peace, on equality. They've even given up on the Democratic Party, which I haven't, not by a long shot. You do what you can, what good people have always done: You bring thirsty people water; you share your food, you try to help the homeless find shelter, you stand up for the underdog.

Anything that can help you get your sense of humor back feeds the spirit, too. In the Bill Murray army movie *Stripes*, a very tense recruit announces during his platoon's introductions,

"My name is Francis. No one calls me Francis. Anyone calls me Francis, I'll kill them. And I don't like to be touched — anyone tries to touch me, I'll kill them." And the sergeant responds, "Oh, lighten up, Francis." So you may need to upgrade your friends. You need to find people who laugh gently at themselves, who remind you gently to lighten up.

Rest and laughter are the most spiritual and subversive acts of all. Laugh, rest, slow down. Some of you start jobs Monday; some of you desperately wish you did — some of your parents are asthmatic with anxiety that you don't. They shared this with me before the ceremony began.

But again, this is not your problem. If your family is hell-bent on you making a name for yourself in the field of, say, molecular cell biology, then maybe when you're giving them a final tour of campus, you can show them to the admissions office. I doubt very seriously that they could even get into U.C. Berkeley — I talked to a professor who said there is not a chance he could get in these days.

So I would recommend that you all just take a long deep breath, and stop. Just be where your butts are, and breathe. Take some time. You are graduating today. Refuse to cooperate with anyone who is trying to shame you into hopping right back up onto the rat exercise wheel.

Rest, but pay attention. Refuse to cooperate with anyone who is stealing your freedom, your personal and civil liberties, and then smirking about it. I'm not going to name names. Just send money to the ACLU whenever you can.

But slow down if you can. Better yet, lie down.

In my twenties I devised a school of relaxation that has unfortunately fallen out of favor in the ensuing years — it was called Prone Yoga. You just lie around as much as possible. You could read, listen to music, you could space out, or sleep. But you had to be lying down. Maintaining the prone.

You've graduated. You have nothing left to prove, and besides, it's a fool's game. If you agree to play, you've already lost. It's Charlie Brown and Lucy, with the football. If you keep getting back on the field, they win. There are so many great things to do right now. Write. Sing. Rest. Eat cherries. Register voters. And — oh my God — I nearly forgot the most important thing: refuse to wear uncomfortable pants, even if they make you look really thin. Promise me you'll never wear pants that bind or tug or hurt, pants that have an opinion about how much you've just eaten. The pants may be lying! There is way too much lying and scolding going on politically right now without your pants getting in on the act, too.

So bless you. You've done an amazing thing. And you are loved; you are capable of lives of great joy and meaning. It's what you are made of. And it's what you're for. So take care of yourselves; take care of each other. Thank you.

The Power of Four

Tom Hanks

TOM HANKS is the winner of two Best Actor Academy Awards for his performances in *Forrest Gump* and *Philadelphia*, and he is one of Hollywood's most versatile and highly respected actors. His other films include such acclaimed successes as *Captain Phillips, Charlie Wilson's War*, *The Da Vinci Code*, *The Polar Express*, *Road to Perdition*, *Cast Away*, *Saving Private Ryan*, *Toy Story*, *Apollo 13*, *Sleepless in Seattle*, and *Big*. Mr. Hanks is also a producer (*Mamma Mia*, *My Big Fat Greek Wedding*), as well as a director and writer (*That Thing You Do*, and episodes of the TV mini-series *Band of Brothers* and *From the Earth to the Moon*).

The Power of Four

Tom Hanks

In his 2005 commencement address at Vassar College, Tom Hanks sheds light on "how a simple choice will make a jaw-dropping difference to our world."

Not long ago I was reading about the problem of gridlock on the freeways of Southern California — the traffic jams which cripple the city, stranding millions and laying waste to time, energy, and the environment. Gridlock is as serious and as impenetrable a problem as any we face, a dilemma without cure, without solution, like everything else in the world, it seems.

Some smart folks concocted a computer simulation of gridlock to determine how many cars should be taken off the road to turn a completely jammed and stilled highway into a free-flowing one. How many cars must be removed from that commute until a twenty-mile drive takes twenty-five minutes instead of two hours? The results were startling.

Four cars needed to be removed from that virtually stuck

highway to free up that simulated commute. . . four cars out of each one hundred. Four cars per one hundred cars, four autos out of every one hundred autos, forty cars from each thousand, four hundred out of ten thousand. Four cars out of one hundred are not that many. Two cars out of every fifty — one driver out of twenty-five drivers.

Now, if this simulation is correct, it is the most dramatic definition in earthly science and human nature of how a simple choice will make a jaw-dropping difference to our world. Call it the Power of Four. One commuter in your neighborhood could put the rush back into rush hour. So, if merely four people out of a hundred can make gridlock go away by choosing not to use their car, imagine the other changes that can be wrought just by four of us — four of you — out of a hundred.

Take a hundred musicians in a depressed port city in Northern England, choose John, Paul, George, and Ringo and you have "Hey Jude." Take a hundred computer geeks in Redmond, Washington, send ninety-six of them home and the remainder is called Microsoft.

Take the Power of Four and apply it to any and every area of your concern. Politics: Four votes swung from one hundred into another hundred is the difference between gaining control and losing clout. Culture: two ticket buyers out of fifty can make a small, odd film profitable. Economics: by boycotting a product one consumer out of twenty-five can move that product to the back of the shelf, and eventually off it altogether.

Four out of one hundred is miniscule and yet can be the great lever of the Tipping Point. The Power of Four is the difference between helplessness and help. H-E-L-P: a four-letter word like some others with many meanings.

The graduating class of 2005 can claim, with perhaps more credibility than any other class in history, that during its four years of college the world went crazy. In the fall of 2001, our planet Earth and the United States of America were different sorts of places — in tone, in tolerance, in peace and war, in ideas and in ideals — than they are on this spring day in 2005.

These past years have been extraordinary in the express rate of change, well beyond the usual standards of culture. You now live in a brand new world, with new versions of political upheaval, global pandemic, world war and religious polarization, the likes of which have rarely visited our planet all at once — and thank God for that.

None of you were untouched by the events in September 2001, none unaffected by the ideological movements of local and geo-politics since. All of you have been staring your individual fate and our collective future right in the eye for the last four years. The common stereotype would have you today, cap in the air, parchment in hand, asking yourself, "What do I do now?" You have already had many, many moments when you asked yourself that question. You might have added the word 'Hell', or some such four-letter word to the phrase: "What the HELL do I do now?" In which case, today might not be all that different from other days on campus — except your parents are here and they might take you out for better food.

On Commencement Day, speechmakers are expected to offer advice — as though you need any, as though anything said today could aid your making sense of our one-damn-thing-after-another world. Things are too confused, too loud, and too dangerous to make 'advice' an option. You need to hear something much more relevant on this day. You need to hear the most important message thus far in the third millennium. You need to hear a maxim so simple, so clear and evocative that no one could misconstrue its meaning or miss its weighty issue.

So, here goes. It's not a statement, but a request. Not a bit of advice, but a plea. It is, in fact, a single four-letter word, a verb and a noun which takes into account the reality of your four years at college as well as the demands of the next four decades you spend beyond this campus.

It's a message, once made familiar by the Beatles — those Northern English lads who embodied The Power of Four.

Help. HELP. HEEEELLLLLPP!

We need help. Your help. You must help. Please help. Please provide Help. Please be willing to help. Help. . . and you will make a huge impact in the life of the street, the town, the country, and our planet. If only one out of four of each one hundred of you choose to help on any given day, in any given cause — incredible things will happen in the world you live in.

Help publicly. Help privately. Help in your actions by recycling and conserving and protecting, but help also in your attitude. Help make sense where sense has gone missing. Help bring reason and respect to discourse and debate. Help science to solve and faith to soothe. Help law bring justice, until justice is commonplace. Help and you will abolish apathy — the void that is so quickly filled by ignorance and evil.

Life outside of college is just like life in it: one nutty thing after another, some of them horrible, but all interspersed with enough beauty and goodness to keep you going. That's your job, to keep going. Your duty is to help — without ceasing. The art you create can glorify it. The science you pursue can prove its value. The law you practice can pass on its benefits. The faith you embrace will make it the earthly manifestation of your God.

Whatever your discipline, whatever your passion, you have already experienced the exhausting reality that there is always something going on and there is always something to do. And most assuredly you have sensed how effective and empowering it can be when more than four out of one hundred make the same choice to help.

You will always be able to help.

So do it. Make peace where it is precious. Help plant trees. Help embrace diversity and celebrate differences. Help stop gridlock.

In other words, help solve every problem we face — every single one of them — with the Power of Four out of a hundred. Help and we will save the world. If we don't help — it won't get done.

Congratulations. Good luck.

About the Editor

Mark Evan Chimsky is the head of Mark Chimsky Editorial Services Unlimited, an editorial consulting business based in Portland, Maine. For nearly six years, he was the editor in chief of the book division of Sellers Publishing, an independent publishing company based in South Portland, Maine. Previously he was executive editor and editorial director of Harper San Francisco and headed the paperback divisions at Little, Brown and Macmillan. In addition, he was on the faculty of New York University's Center for Publishing, and for three years he served as the director of the book section of NYU's Summer Publishing Institute. He has edited a number of best-selling books, including Johnny Cash's memoir, *Cash*, and he has worked with such notable authors as Melody Beattie, Arthur Hertzberg, Beryl Bender Birch, and Robert Coles. He was also project manager on Billy Graham's *New York Times* best-selling memoir, *Just As I Am*. He conceived of the long-running series *The Best American Erotica*, which was compiled by Susie Bright, and he was the first editor to reissue the works of celebrated novelist Dawn Powell. His editorial achievements have been noted in *Vanity Fair*, the *Nation*, and *Publishers Weekly*. He is an award-winning poet whose poetry and essays have appeared in *JAMA* (the *Journal of the American Medical Association*), *Wild Violet*, *Three Rivers Poetry Journal*, and *Mississippi Review*. For Sellers Publishing, he developed and compiled a number of acclaimed books, including *Creating a Life You'll Love*, which won the silver in *ForeWord's* 2009 Book of the Year Awards (self-help category), *65 Things to Do When You Retire*, which the *Wall Street Journal* called "[one] of the year's best guides to later life," and *65 Things to Do When You Retire: Travel.*

Acknowledgments

I want to first thank all of the contributors whose wonderful commencement addresses appear in this book. They generously agreed to donate their speeches free of charge so that the royalties from the sale of this book can be given to nonprofit organizations dedicated to cancer research and prevention.

I also want to express my deep appreciation to the following individuals who work with or represent the contributors — their efforts helped make this book happen: Lena Auerbuch, Nanda Barker-Hook, Cristina Concepcion, Frederick T. Courtright, Harlene Conley, Vianny Cruz, Frances Goldin, Lina Granada, Dan Green, Charles Greene, Valerie Hamra, Erik Hyman, Morton L. Janklow, Alexia Koch, Julia Masnik, Lamiya Morshed, Eric Price, Rosie Price, Lauren Rogoff, Amanda Schumacher, Michael Steger, and Sam Stoloff.

Thanks as well to Ronnie Sellers, Robin Haywood, Mary Baldwin, Charlotte Cromwell, Diana Kipp, Cynthia Kurtz, Andy Sturtevant, Jo Ann Van Reenen, and Patti Urban.

A shout out to my parents, for encouraging me to share their love of literature; to my brother Rob and sister-in-law Nancy, for all their support; and to my son, the newest writer in the family.

And last but certainly not least, a special debt of gratitude to Laurie Moore Skillings and Kimberly Gladman for more than words can say.

Credits:

"How to be Hopeful," © 2009 Barbara Kingsolver; "The Love of Learning," © 2008 David McCullough; "On Our Relationship with Technology, with the World, and with Ourselves," © 2015 Arianna Huffington; "Go Forth Unafraid," © 2009 The Mary T. Ivins Estate; "Listen to Your Heart," Reprinted by permission of International Creative Management, Inc. © 2005 by Thomas L. Friedman. All rights reserved; The poem "What Teachers Make" appears in Thomas L. Friedman's commencement address by kind permission of the author Taylor Mali; "What I Learned," from *When You Are Engulfed in Flames* by David Sedaris. Copyright © 2006, 2008 by David Sedaris. Reprinted by permission of Little, Brown and Company. All rights reserved; "The Reach," © 2009 Anna Deavere Smith; "You Are Not Alone," © 2009 International Bridges to Justice; The benediction "Take Courage, Friends" appears in Karen Tse's commencement address by kind permission of the author Wayne Arnason; "Speaking Freely," Copyright © Ian McEwan 2015. Reproduced by permission of the author c/o Rogers, Coleridge & White Ltd., 20 Powis Mews, London W11 1JN; "'Be Naked as Often as Possible': Anthropological Advice," © 2009 Genevieve Bell; "What the Future Will Bring," © 2005 Kurzweilai.net; "The Impoverishment of American Culture," © Dana Gioia, June 17, 2007, Stanford University; "Commencement Address," © 2009 Dr. Muhammad Yunus; "The Virtue of Varied Perspectives," International copyright © 2015 U.S. Department of Commerce, U.S. Government; "With Apologies to the Gettysburg Address: May 20, 2007," © 2009 Harold Prince; "Resist!," © 2009 Wendell Berry; "High Stakes," commencement address at Bates College; copyright © 2004 by David Levering Lewis. Used by permission of Brandt & Hochman Literary Agents, Inc.; "The Creepy Biological Facts of Life," © 2009 Tess Gerritsen; "Be Not Afraid," Reprinted by permission of International Creative Management, Inc. © 2006 by Anna Quindlen. All rights reserved; "Let Us Commence," Copyright © 2003 by Anne Lamott, used with permission of The Wylie Agency LLC; "The Power of Four," © 2009 Tom Hanks